17.99

97 Things

Every Programmer Should Know

Collective Wisdom from the Experts

Edited by Kevlin Henney

O'REILLY®

Beijing · Cambridge · Farnham · Köln · Sebastopol · Tokyo

97 Things Every Programmer Should Know
Edited by Kevlin Henney

Published by O'Reilly Media, Inc. 1005 Gravenstein Highway North, Sebastopol CA 95472

O'Reilly books may be purchased for educational, business, or sales promotional use. Online editions are also available for most titles (*http://my.safaribooksonline.com*). For more information, contact our corporate/institutional sales department: (800) 998-9938 or *corporate@oreilly.com*.

Editor: Mike Loukides

Series Editor: Richard Monson-Haefel

Production Editor: Rachel Monaghan

Proofreader: Rachel Monaghan

Compositor: Ron Bilodeau

Indexer: Julie Hawks

Interior Designer: Ron Bilodeau

Cover Designers: Mark Paglietti and Susan Thompson

Print History:

February 2010:   First Edition.

ISBN: 978-0-596-80948-5

To absent friends

Contents

Contributions
by Category

Bugs and Fixes

Build and Deployment

Coding Guidelines and Code Layout

Design Principles and Coding Techniques

Domain Thinking

Errors, Error Handling, and Exceptions

Learning, Skills, and Expertise

Nocturnal or Magical

Performance, Optimization, and Representation

Professionalism, Mindset, and Attitude

Programming Languages and Paradigms

Refactoring and Code Care

Reuse Versus Repetition

Schedules, Deadlines, and Estimates

Simplicity

Teamwork and Collaboration

Tests, Testing, and Testers

Tools, Automation, and Development Environments

Users and Customers

Preface

The newest computer can merely compound, at speed, the oldest problem in the relations between human beings, and in the end the communicator will be confronted with the old problem, of what to say and how to say it.
—Edward R. Murrow

PROGRAMMERS HAVE A LOT ON THEIR MINDS. Programming languages, programming techniques, development environments, coding style, tools, development process, deadlines, meetings, software architecture, design patterns, team dynamics, code, requirements, bugs, code quality. And more. A lot.

There is an art, craft, and science to programming that extends far beyond the program. The act of programming marries the discrete world of computers with the fluid world of human affairs. Programmers mediate between the negotiated and uncertain truths of business and the crisp, uncompromising domain of bits and bytes and higher constructed types.

With so much to know, so much to do, and so many ways of doing so, no single person or single source can lay claim to "the one true way." Instead, *97 Things Every Programmer Should Know* draws on the wisdom of crowds and the voices of experience to offer not so much a coordinated big picture as a crowdsourced mosaic of what every programmer should know. This ranges from code-focused advice to culture, from algorithm usage to agile thinking, from implementation know-how to professionalism, from style to substance.

The contributions do not dovetail like modular parts, and there is no intent that they should—if anything, the opposite is true. The value of each contribution comes from its distinctiveness. The value of the collection lies in how the contributions complement, confirm, and even contradict one another. There is no overarching narrative: it is for you to respond to, reflect on, and connect together what you read, weighing it against your own context, knowledge, and experience.

Permissions

The licensing of each contribution follows a nonrestrictive, open source model. Every contribution is freely available online and licensed under a Creative Commons Attribution 3.0 License, which means that you can use the individual contributions in your own work, as long as you give credit to the original author:

> *http://creativecommons.org/licenses/by/3.0/us/*

How to Contact Us

Please address comments and questions concerning this book to the publisher:

O'Reilly Media, Inc.
1005 Gravenstein Highway North
Sebastopol, CA 95472
800-998-9938 (in the United States or Canada)
707-829-0515 (international or local)
707-829-0104 (fax)

On the web page for this book, we list errata and any additional information. You can access this page at:

> *http://www.oreilly.com/catalog/9780596809485/*

The companion website for this book, where you can find all the contributions, contributor biographies, and more, is at:

> *http://programmer.97things.oreilly.com*

You can also follow news and updates about this book and the website on Twitter:

> *http://twitter.com/97TEPSK*

To comment or ask technical questions about this book, send email to:

> *bookquestions@oreilly.com*

For more information about our books, conferences, Resource Centers, and the O'Reilly Network, see our website at:

> *http://www.oreilly.com/*

Safari® Books Online

 Safari Books Online is an on-demand digital library that lets you easily search over 7,500 technology and creative reference books and videos to find the answers you need quickly.

With a subscription, you can read any page and watch any video from our library online. Read books on your cell phone and mobile devices. Access new titles before they are available for print, and get exclusive access to manuscripts in development and post feedback for the authors. Copy and paste code samples, organize your favorites, download chapters, bookmark key sections, create notes, print out pages, and benefit from tons of other time-saving features.

O'Reilly Media has uploaded this book to the Safari Books Online service. To have full digital access to this book and others on similar topics from O'Reilly and other publishers, sign up for free at *http://my.safaribooksonline.com*.

Acknowledgments

Many people have contributed their time and their insight, both directly and indirectly, to the *97 Things Every Programmer Should Know* project. They all deserve credit.

Richard Monson-Haefel is the 97 Things series editor and also the editor of the first book in the series, *97 Things Every Software Architect Should Know*, to which I contributed. I would like to thank Richard for trailblazing the series concept and its open contribution approach, and for enthusiastically supporting my proposal for this book.

I would like to thank all those who devoted the time and effort to contribute items to this project: both the contributors whose items are published in this book and the others whose items were not selected, but whose items are also published on the website. The high quantity and quality of contributions made the final selection process very difficult—the hardcoded number in the book's title unfortunately meant there was no slack to accommodate just a few more. I am also grateful for the additional feedback, comments, and suggestions provided by Giovanni Asproni, Paul Colin Gloster, and Michael Hunger.

Thanks to O'Reilly for the support they have provided this project, from hosting the wiki that made it possible to seeing it all the way through to publication in book form. People at O'Reilly I would like to thank specifically are Mike Loukides, Laurel Ackerman, Edie Freedman, Ed Stephenson, and Rachel Monaghan.

It is not simply the case that the book's content was developed on the Web: the project was also publicized and popularized on the Web. I would like to thank all those who have tweeted, retweeted, blogged, and otherwise spread the word.

I would also like to thank my wife, Carolyn, for bringing order to my chaos, and to my two sons, Stefan and Yannick, for reclaiming some of the chaos.

I hope this book will provide you with information, insight, and inspiration.

Enjoy!

—Kevlin Henney

Act with Prudence

Seb Rose

> *Whatever you undertake, act with prudence and consider the consequences.*
>
> —Anon

NO MATTER HOW COMFORTABLE A SCHEDULE LOOKS at the beginning of an iteration, you can't avoid being under pressure some of the time. If you find yourself having to choose between "doing it right" and "doing it quick," it is often appealing to "do it quick" with the understanding that you'll come back and fix it later. When you make this promise to yourself, your team, and your customer, you mean it. But all too often, the next iteration brings new problems and you become focused on them. This sort of deferred work is known as *technical debt*, and it is not your friend. Specifically, Martin Fowler calls this *deliberate technical debt* in his taxonomy of technical debt,* and it should not be confused with *inadvertent technical debt*.

Technical debt is like a loan: you benefit from it in the short term, but you have to pay interest on it until it is fully paid off. Shortcuts in the code make it harder to add features or refactor your code. They are breeding grounds for defects and brittle test cases. The longer you leave it, the worse it gets. By the time you get around to undertaking the original fix, there may be a whole stack of not-quite-right design choices layered on top of the original problem, making the code much harder to refactor and correct. In fact, it is often only when things have got so bad that you *must* fix the original problem, that you actually do go back to fix it. And by then, it is often so hard to fix that you really can't afford the time or the risk.

---

* *http://martinfowler.com/bliki/TechnicalDebtQuadrant.html*

There are times when you must incur technical debt to meet a deadline or implement a thin slice of a feature. Try not to be in this position, but if the situation absolutely demands it, then go ahead. But (and this is a big *but*) you must track technical debt and pay it back quickly, or things go rapidly downhill. As soon as you make the decision to compromise, write a task card or log it in your issue-tracking system to ensure that it does not get forgotten.

If you schedule repayment of the debt in the next iteration, the cost will be minimal. Leaving the debt unpaid will accrue interest, and that interest should be tracked to make the cost visible. This will emphasize the effect on business value of the project's technical debt and enables appropriate prioritization of the repayment. The choice of how to calculate and track the interest will depend on the particular project, but track it you must.

Pay off technical debt as soon as possible. It would be imprudent to do otherwise.

Apply Functional Programming Principles

Edward Garson

FUNCTIONAL PROGRAMMING has recently enjoyed renewed interest from the mainstream programming community. Part of the reason is because *emergent properties* of the functional paradigm are well positioned to address the challenges posed by our industry's shift toward multicore. However, while that is certainly an important application, it is not the reason this piece admonishes you to *know thy functional programming*.

Mastery of the functional programming paradigm can greatly improve the quality of the code you write in other contexts. If you deeply understand and apply the functional paradigm, your designs will exhibit a much higher degree of *referential transparency*.

Referential transparency is a very desirable property: it implies that functions consistently yield the same results given the same input, irrespective of where and when they are invoked. That is, function evaluation depends less—ideally, not at all—on the side effects of mutable state.

A leading cause of defects in imperative code is attributable to mutable variables. Everyone reading this will have investigated why some value is not as expected in a particular situation. Visibility semantics can help to mitigate these insidious defects, or at least to drastically narrow down their location, but their true culprit may in fact be the providence of designs that employ inordinate mutability.

And we certainly don't get much help from the industry in this regard. Introductions to object orientation tacitly promote such design, because they often show examples composed of graphs of relatively long-lived objects that happily call mutator methods on one another, which can be dangerous.

However, with astute test-driven design, particularly when being sure to "Mock Roles, not Objects,"* unnecessary mutability can be designed away.

The net result is a design that typically has better responsibility allocation with more numerous, smaller functions that act on arguments passed into them, rather than referencing mutable member variables. There will be fewer defects, and furthermore they will often be simpler to debug, because it is easier to locate where a rogue value is introduced in these designs than to otherwise deduce the particular context that results in an erroneous assignment. This adds up to a *much higher degree* of referential transparency, and positively nothing will get these ideas as deeply into your bones as learning a functional programming language, where this model of computation is the norm.

Of course, this approach is not optimal in all situations. For example, in object-oriented systems, this style often yields better results with domain model development (i.e., where collaborations serve to break down the complexity of business rules) than with user-interface development.

Master the functional programming paradigm so you are able to judiciously apply the lessons learned to other domains. Your object systems (for one) will resonate with referential transparency goodness and be much closer to their functional counterparts than many would have you believe. In fact, some would even assert that, at their apex, functional programming and object orientation are *merely a reflection of each other*, a form of computational yin and yang.

* *http://www.jmock.org/oopsla2004.pdf*

Ask, "What Would the User Do?" (You Are Not the User)

Giles Colborne

WE ALL TEND TO ASSUME THAT OTHER PEOPLE THINK LIKE US. But they don't. Psychologists call this the *false consensus bias*. When people think or act differently from us, we're quite likely to label them (subconsciously) as defective in some way.

This bias explains why programmers have such a hard time putting themselves in the users' position. Users don't think like programmers. For a start, they spend much less time using computers. They neither know nor care how a computer works. This means they can't draw on any of the battery of problem-solving techniques so familiar to programmers. They don't recognize the patterns and cues programmers use to work with, through, and around an interface.

The best way to find out how a user thinks is to watch one. Ask a user to complete a task using a similar piece of software to what you're developing. Make sure the task is a real one: "Add up a column of numbers" is OK; "Calculate your expenses for the last month" is better. Avoid tasks that are too specific, such as "Can you select these spreadsheet cells and enter a *SUM* formula below?"—there's a big clue in that question. Get the user to talk through his or her progress. Don't interrupt. Don't try to help. Keep asking yourself, "Why is he doing that?" and "Why is she not doing that?"

The first thing you'll notice is that users do a core of things similarly. They try to complete tasks in the same order—and they make the same mistakes in the same places. You should design around that core behavior. This is different from design meetings, where people tend to listen when someone says, "What if the user wants to…?" This leads to elaborate features and confusion over what users want. Watching users eliminates this confusion.

You'll see users getting stuck. When you get stuck, you look around. When users get stuck, they narrow their focus. It becomes harder for them to see solutions elsewhere on the screen. It's one reason why help text is a poor solution to poor user interface design. If you must have instructions or help text, make sure to locate it right next to your problem areas. A user's narrow focus of attention is why tool tips are more useful than help menus.

Users tend to muddle through. They'll find a way that works and stick with it, no matter how convoluted. It's better to provide one really obvious way of doing things than two or three shortcuts.

You'll also find that there's a gap between what users say they want and what they actually do. That's worrying, as the normal way of gathering user requirements is to ask them. It's why the best way to capture requirements is to watch users. Spending an hour watching users is more informative than spending a day guessing what they want.

Automate Your
Coding Standard

Filip van Laenen

YOU'VE PROBABLY BEEN THERE, TOO. At the beginning of a project, everybody has lots of good intentions—call them "new project's resolutions." Quite often, many of these resolutions are written down in documents. The ones about code end up in the project's coding standard. During the kick-off meeting, the lead developer goes through the document and, in the best case, everybody agrees that they will try to follow them. Once the project gets underway, though, these good intentions are abandoned, one at a time. When the project is finally delivered, the code looks like a mess, and nobody seems to know how it came to be that way.

When did things go wrong? Probably already at the kick-off meeting. Some of the project members didn't pay attention. Others didn't understand the point. Worse, some disagreed and were already planning their coding standard rebellion. Finally, some got the point and agreed, but when the pressure in the project got too high, they had to let something go. Well-formatted code doesn't earn you points with a customer that wants more functionality. Furthermore, following a coding standard can be quite a boring task if it isn't automated. Just try to indent a messy class by hand to find out for yourself.

But if it's such a problem, why is it that we want a coding standard in the first place? One reason to format the code in a uniform way is so that nobody can "own" a piece of code just by formatting it in his or her private way. We may want to prevent developers from using certain antipatterns in order to avoid some common bugs. In all, a coding standard should make it easier to work in the project, and maintain development speed from the beginning to the end. It follows, then, that everybody should agree on the coding standard, too—it does not help if one developer uses three spaces to indent code, and another uses four.

There exists a wealth of tools that can be used to produce code quality reports and to document and maintain the coding standard, but that isn't the whole solution. It should be automated and enforced where possible. Here are a few examples:

- Make sure code formatting is part of the build process, so that everybody runs it automatically every time they compile the code.

- Use static code analysis tools to scan the code for unwanted antipatterns. If any are found, break the build.

- Learn to configure those tools so that you can scan for your own, project-specific antipatterns.

- Do not only measure test coverage, but automatically check the results, too. Again, break the build if test coverage is too low.

Try to do this for everything that you consider important. You won't be able to automate everything you really care about. As for the things that you can't automatically flag or fix, consider them a set of guidelines supplementary to the coding standard that is automated, but accept that you and your colleagues may not follow them as diligently.

Finally, the coding standard should be dynamic rather than static. As the project evolves, the needs of the project change, and what may have seemed smart in the beginning isn't necessarily smart a few months later.

Beauty Is in Simplicity

Jørn Ølmheim

THERE IS ONE QUOTE, from Plato, that I think is particularly good for all software developers to know and keep close to their hearts:

> *Beauty of style and harmony and grace and good rhythm depends on simplicity.*

In one sentence, this sums up the values that we as software developers should aspire to.

There are a number of things we strive for in our code:

- Readability

- Maintainability

- Speed of development

- The elusive quality of beauty

Plato is telling us that the enabling factor for all of these qualities is simplicity.

What is beautiful code? This is potentially a very subjective question. Perception of beauty depends heavily on individual background, just as much of our perception of anything depends on our background. People educated in the arts have a different perception of (or at least approach to) beauty than people educated in the sciences. Arts majors tend to approach beauty in software by comparing software to works of art, while science majors tend to talk about symmetry and the golden ratio, trying to reduce things to formulae. In my experience, simplicity is the foundation of most of the arguments from both sides.

Think about source code that you have studied. If you haven't spent time studying other people's code, stop reading this right now and find some open source code to study. Seriously! I mean it! Go search the Web for some code in your language of choice, written by some well-known, acknowledged expert.

You're back? Good. Where were we? Ah, yes...I have found that code that resonates with me, and that I consider beautiful, has a number of properties in common. Chief among these is simplicity. I find that no matter how complex the total application or system is, the individual parts have to be kept simple: simple objects with a single responsibility containing similarly simple, focused methods with descriptive names. Some people think the idea of having short methods of 5–10 lines of code is extreme, and some languages make it very hard to do, but I think that such brevity is a desirable goal nonetheless.

The bottom line is that beautiful code is simple code. Each individual part is kept simple with simple responsibilities and simple relationships with the other parts of the system. This is the way we can keep our systems maintainable over time, with clean, simple, testable code, ensuring a high speed of development throughout the lifetime of the system.

Beauty is born of and found in simplicity.

Before You Refactor

Rajith Attapattu

AT SOME POINT, every programmer will need to refactor existing code. But before you do so, please think about the following, as this could save you and others a great deal of time (and pain):

- *The best approach for restructuring starts by taking stock of the existing codebase and the tests written against that code.* This will help you understand the strengths and weaknesses of the code as it currently stands, so you can ensure that you retain the strong points while avoiding the mistakes. We all think we can do better than the existing system…until we end up with something no better—or even worse—than the previous incarnation because we failed to learn from the existing system's mistakes.

- *Avoid the temptation to rewrite everything.* It is best to reuse as much code as possible. No matter how ugly the code is, it has already been tested, reviewed, etc. Throwing away the old code—especially if it was in production—means that you are throwing away months (or years) of tested, battle-hardened code that may have had certain workarounds and bug fixes you aren't aware of. If you don't take this into account, the new code you write may end up showing the same mysterious bugs that were fixed in the old code. This will waste a lot of time, effort, and knowledge gained over the years.

- *Many incremental changes are better than one massive change.* Incremental changes allows you to gauge the impact on the system more easily through feedback, such as from tests. It is no fun to see a hundred test failures after you make a change. This can lead to frustration and pressure that can in turn result in bad decisions. A couple of test failures at a time is easier to deal with, leading to a more manageable approach.

- *After each development iteration, it is important to ensure that the existing tests pass.* Add new tests if the existing tests are not sufficient to cover the changes you made. Do not throw away the tests from the old code without due consideration. On the surface, some of these tests may not appear to be applicable to your new design, but it would be well worth the effort to dig deep down into the reasons why this particular test was added.

- *Personal preferences and ego shouldn't get in the way.* If something isn't broken, why fix it? That the style or the structure of the code does not meet your personal preference is not a valid reason for restructuring. Thinking you could do a better job than the previous programmer is not a valid reason, either.

- *New technology is an insufficient reason to refactor.* One of the worst reasons to refactor is because the current code is way behind all the cool technology we have today, and we believe that a new language or framework can do things a lot more elegantly. Unless a cost-benefit analysis shows that a new language or framework will result in significant improvements in functionality, maintainability, or productivity, it is best to leave it as it is.

- *Remember that humans make mistakes.* Restructuring will not always guarantee that the new code will be better—or even as good as—the previous attempt. I have seen and been a part of several failed restructuring attempts. It wasn't pretty, but it was human.

Beware the Share

Udi Dahan

IT WAS MY FIRST PROJECT AT THE COMPANY. I'd just finished my degree and was anxious to prove myself, staying late every day going through the existing code. As I worked through my first feature, I took extra care to put in place everything I had learned—commenting, logging, pulling out shared code into libraries where possible, the works. The code review that I had felt so ready for came as a rude awakening—reuse was frowned upon!

How could this be? Throughout college, reuse was held up as the epitome of quality software engineering. All the articles I had read, the textbooks, the seasoned software professionals who taught me—was it all wrong?

It turns out that I was missing something critical.

Context.

The fact that two wildly different parts of the system performed some logic in the same way meant less than I thought. Up until I had pulled out those libraries of shared code, these parts were not dependent on each other. Each could evolve independently. Each could change its logic to suit the needs of the system's changing business environment. Those four lines of similar code were accidental—a temporal anomaly, a coincidence. That is, until I came along.

The libraries of shared code I created tied the shoelaces of each foot to the other. Steps by one business domain could not be made without first synchronizing with the other. Maintenance costs in those independent functions used to be negligible, but the common library required an order of magnitude more testing.

While I'd decreased the absolute number of lines of code in the system, I had increased the number of dependencies. The context of these dependencies is critical—had they been localized, the sharing may have been justified and had some positive value. When these dependencies aren't held in check, their tendrils entangle the larger concerns of the system, even though the code itself looks just fine.

These mistakes are insidious in that, at their core, they sound like a good idea. When applied in the right context, these techniques are valuable. In the wrong context, they increase cost rather than value. When coming into an existing codebase with no knowledge of where the various parts will be used, I'm much more careful these days about what is shared.

Beware the share. Check your context. Only then, proceed.

The Boy Scout Rule

Robert C. Martin (Uncle Bob)

THE BOY SCOUTS HAVE A RULE: "Always leave the campground cleaner than you found it." If you find a mess on the ground, you clean it up regardless of who might have made it. You intentionally improve the environment for the next group of campers. (Actually, the original form of that rule, written by Robert Stephenson Smyth Baden-Powell, the father of scouting, was "Try and leave this world a little better than you found it.")

What if we followed a similar rule in our code: "Always check a module in cleaner than when you checked it out"? Regardless of who the original author was, what if we always made some effort, no matter how small, to improve the module? What would be the result?

I think if we all followed that simple rule, we would see the end of the relentless deterioration of our software systems. Instead, our systems would gradually get better and better as they evolved. We would also see *teams* caring for the system as a whole, rather than just individuals caring for their own small part.

I don't think this rule is too much to ask. You don't have to make every module perfect before you check it in. You simply have to make it *a little bit better* than when you checked it out. Of course, this means that any code you *add* to a module must be clean. It also means that you clean up at least one other thing before you check the module back in. You might simply improve the name of one variable, or split one long function into two smaller functions. You might break a circular dependency, or add an interface to decouple policy from detail.

Frankly, this just sounds like common decency to me—like washing your hands after you use the restroom, or putting your trash in the bin instead of dropping it on the floor. Indeed, the act of leaving a mess in the code should be as socially unacceptable as littering. It should be something that *just isn't done*.

But it's more than that. Caring for our own code is one thing. Caring for the *team*'s code is quite another. Teams help one another and clean up after one another. They follow the Boy Scout rule because it's good for everyone, not just good for themselves.

Check Your Code
First Before Looking
to Blame Others

Allan Kelly

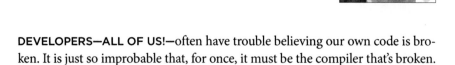

DEVELOPERS—ALL OF US!—often have trouble believing our own code is broken. It is just so improbable that, for once, it must be the compiler that's broken.

Yet, in truth, it is very (very) unusual that code is broken by a bug in the compiler, interpreter, OS, app server, database, memory manager, or any other piece of system software. Yes, these bugs exist, but they are far less common than we might like to believe.

I once had a genuine problem with a compiler bug optimizing away a loop variable, but I have imagined my compiler or OS had a bug many more times. I have wasted a lot of my time, support time, and management time in the process, only to feel a little foolish each time it turned out to be my mistake after all.

Assuming that the tools are widely used, mature, and employed in various technology stacks, there is little reason to doubt the quality. Of course, if the tool is an early release, or used by only a few people worldwide, or a piece of seldom downloaded, version 0.1, open source software, there may be good reason to suspect the software. (Equally, an alpha version of commercial software might be suspect.)

Given how rare compiler bugs are, you are far better putting your time and energy into finding the error in your code than into proving that the compiler is wrong. All the usual debugging advice applies, so isolate the problem, stub out calls, and surround it with tests; check calling conventions, shared libraries, and version numbers; explain it to someone else; look out for stack corruption and variable type mismatches; and try the code on different machines and different build configurations, such as debug and release.

Question your own assumptions and the assumptions of others. Tools from different vendors might have different assumptions built into them—so too might different tools from the same vendor.

When someone else is reporting a problem you cannot duplicate, go and see what they are doing. They may be doing something you never thought of or are doing something in a different order.

My personal rule is that if I have a bug I can't pin down, and I'm starting to think it's the compiler, then it's time to look for stack corruption. This is especially true if adding trace code makes the problem move around.

Multithreaded problems are another source of bugs that turn hair gray and induce screaming at the machine. All the recommendations to favor simple code are multiplied when a system is multithreaded. Debugging and unit tests cannot be relied on to find such bugs with any consistency, so simplicity of design is paramount.

So, before you rush to blame the compiler, remember Sherlock Holmes's advice, "Once you eliminate the impossible, whatever remains, no matter how improbable, must be the truth," and opt for it over Dirk Gently's, "Once you eliminate the improbable, whatever remains, no matter how impossible, must be the truth."

Choose Your Tools with Care

Giovanni Asproni

MODERN APPLICATIONS ARE VERY RARELY BUILT FROM SCRATCH. They are assembled using existing tools—components, libraries, and frameworks—for a number of good reasons:

- Applications grow in size, complexity, and sophistication, while the time available to develop them grows shorter. It makes better use of developers' time and intelligence if they can concentrate on writing more business-domain code and less infrastructure code.

- Widely used components and frameworks are likely to have fewer bugs than the ones developed in-house.

- There is a lot of high-quality software available on the Web for free, which means lower development costs and greater likelihood of finding developers with the necessary interest and expertise.

- Software production and maintenance is human-intensive work, so buying may be cheaper than building.

However, choosing the right mix of tools for your application can be a tricky business requiring some thought. In fact, when making a choice, you should keep in mind a few things:

- Different tools may rely on different assumptions about their context—e.g., surrounding infrastructure, control model, data model, communication protocols, etc.—which can lead to an *architectural mismatch* between the application and the tools. Such a mismatch leads to hacks and workarounds that will make the code more complex than necessary.

- Different tools have different lifecycles, and upgrading one of them may become an extremely difficult and time-consuming task since the new functionality, design changes, or even bug fixes may cause incompatibilities with the other tools. The greater the number of tools, the worse the problem can become.

- Some tools require quite a bit of configuration, often by means of one or more XML files, which can grow out of control very quickly. The application may end up looking as if it was all written in XML plus a few odd lines of code in some programming language. The configurational complexity will make the application difficult to maintain and to extend.

- Vendor lock-in occurs when code that depends heavily on specific vendor products ends up being constrained by them on several counts: maintainability, performances, ability to evolve, price, etc.

- If you plan to use free software, you may discover that it's not so free after all. You may need to buy commercial support, which is not necessarily going to be cheap.

- Licensing terms matter, even for free software. For example, in some companies, it is not acceptable to use software licensed under the GNU license terms because of its viral nature—i.e., software developed with it must be distributed along with its source code.

My personal strategy to mitigate these problems is to start small by using only the tools that are absolutely necessary. Usually the initial focus is on removing the need to engage in low-level infrastructure programming (and problems), e.g., by using some middleware instead of using raw sockets for distributed applications. And then add more if needed. I also tend to isolate the external tools from my business domain objects by means of interfaces and layering, so that I can change the tool if I have to with a minimal amount of pain. A positive side effect of this approach is that I generally end up with a smaller application that uses fewer external tools than originally forecast.

Code in the Language of the Domain

Dan North

PICTURE TWO CODEBASES. In one, you come across:

```
if (portfolioIdsByTraderId.get(trader.getId())
    .containsKey(portfolio.getId())) {...}
```

You scratch your head, wondering what this code might be for. It seems to be getting an ID from a trader object; using that to get a map out of a, well, map-of-maps, apparently; and then seeing if another ID from a portfolio object exists in the inner map. You scratch your head some more. You look for the declaration of portfolioIdsByTraderId and discover this:

```
Map<int, Map<int, int>> portfolioIdsByTraderId;
```

Gradually, you realize it might have something to do with whether a trader has access to a particular portfolio. And of course you will find the same lookup fragment—or, more likely, a similar but subtly different code fragment—whenever something cares whether a trader has access to a particular portfolio.

In the other codebase, you come across this:

```
if (trader.canView(portfolio)) {...}
```

No head scratching. You don't need to know how a trader knows. Perhaps there is one of these maps-of-maps tucked away somewhere inside. But that's the trader's business, not yours.

Now which of those codebases would you rather be working in?

Once upon a time, we only had very basic data structures: bits and bytes and characters (really just bytes, but we would pretend they were letters and punctuation). Decimals were a bit tricky because our base-10 numbers don't work very well in binary, so we had several sizes of floating-point types. Then came arrays and strings (really just different arrays). Then we had stacks and queues and hashes and linked lists and skip lists and lots of other exciting data structures that *don't exist in the real world*. "Computer science" was about spending lots of effort mapping the real world into our restrictive data structures. The real gurus could even remember how they had done it.

Then we got user-defined types! OK, this isn't news, but it does change the game somewhat. If your domain contains concepts like traders and portfolios, you can model them with types called, say, Trader and Portfolio. But, more importantly than this, you can model *relationships between them* using domain terms, too.

If you don't code using domain terms, you are creating a tacit (read: secret) understanding that *this* int over here means the way to identify a trader, whereas *that* int over there means the way to identify a portfolio. (Best not to get them mixed up!) And if you represent a business concept ("Some traders are not allowed to view some portfolios—it's illegal") with an algorithmic snippet—say, an existence relationship in a map of keys—you aren't doing the audit and compliance guys any favors.

The next programmer to come along might not be in on the secret, so why not make it explicit? Using a key as a lookup to another key that performs an existence check is not terribly obvious. How is someone supposed to intuit that's where the business rules preventing conflict of interest are implemented?

Making domain concepts explicit in your code means other programmers can gather the intent of the code much more easily than by trying to retrofit an algorithm into what they understand about a domain. It also means that when the domain model evolves—which it will, as your understanding of the domain grows—you are in a good position to evolve the code. Coupled with good encapsulation, the chances are good that the rule will exist in only one place, and that you can change it without any of the dependent code being any the wiser.

The programmer who comes along a few months later to work on the code will thank you. The programmer who comes along a few months later might be you.

Code Is Design

Ryan Brush

IMAGINE WAKING UP TOMORROW and learning that the construction industry has made the breakthrough of the century. Millions of cheap, incredibly
fast robots can fabricate materials out of thin air, have a near-zero power cost,
and can repair themselves. And it gets better: given an unambiguous blueprint
for a construction project, the robots can build it without human intervention,
all at negligible cost.

One can imagine the impact on the construction industry, but what would
happen upstream? How would the behavior of architects and designers change
if construction costs were negligible? Today, physical and computer models are
built and rigorously tested before investing in construction. Would we bother
if the construction was essentially free? If a design collapses, no big deal—just
find out what went wrong and have our magical robots build another one.
There are further implications. With models obsolete, unfinished designs
evolve by repeatedly building and improving upon an approximation of the
end goal. A casual observer may have trouble distinguishing an unfinished
design from a finished product.

Our ability to predict timelines will fade away. Construction costs are more
easily calculated than design costs—we know the approximate cost of install-
ing a girder, and how many girders we need. As predictable tasks shrink toward
zero, the less predictable design time starts to dominate. Results are produced
more quickly, but reliable timelines slip away.

Of course, the pressures of a competitive economy still apply. With construction costs eliminated, a company that can quickly complete a design gains an

edge in the market. Getting design done fast becomes the central push of engineering firms. Inevitably, someone not deeply familiar with the design will see an unvalidated version, see the market advantage of releasing early, and say, "This looks good enough."

Some life-or-death projects will be more diligent, but in many cases, consumers learn to suffer through the incomplete design. Companies can always send out our magic robots to "patch" the broken buildings and vehicles they sell. All of this points to a startlingly counterintuitive conclusion: our sole premise was a dramatic reduction in construction costs, with the result that *quality got worse*.

It shouldn't surprise us that the preceding story has played out in software. If we accept that code is design—a creative process rather than a mechanical one—the *software crisis* is explained. We now have a *design crisis*: the demand for quality, validated designs exceeds our capacity to create them. The pressure to use incomplete design is strong.

Fortunately, this model also offers clues to how we can get better. Physical simulations equate to automated testing; software design isn't complete until it is validated with a brutal battery of tests. To make such tests more effective, we are finding ways to rein in the huge state space of large systems. Improved languages and design practices give us hope. Finally, there is one inescapable fact: great designs are produced by great designers dedicating themselves to the mastery of their craft. Code is no different.

Code Layout Matters

Steve Freeman

AN INFEASIBLE NUMBER OF YEARS AGO, I worked on a Cobol system where staff members weren't allowed to change the indentation unless they already had a reason to change the code, because someone once broke something by letting a line slip into one of the special columns at the beginning of a line. This applied even if the layout was misleading, which it sometimes was, so we had to read the code very carefully because we couldn't trust it. The policy must have cost a fortune in programmer drag.

There's research suggesting that we all spend much more of our programming time navigating and reading code—finding *where* to make the change—than actually typing, so that's what we want to optimize for. Here are three such optimizations:

Easy to scan

People are really good at visual pattern matching (a leftover trait from the time when we had to spot lions on the savannah), so I can help myself by making everything that isn't directly relevant to the domain—all the "accidental complexity" that comes with most commercial languages— fade into the background by standardizing it. If code that behaves the same looks the same, then my perceptual system will help me pick out the differences. That's why I also observe conventions about how to lay out the parts of a class within a compilation unit: constants, fields, public methods, private methods.

Expressive layout

We've all learned to take the time to find the right names so that our code expresses as clearly as possible what it does, rather than just listing the steps—right? The code's layout is part of this expressiveness, too. A first cut is to have the team agree on an automatic formatter for the basics, and then I might make adjustments by hand while I'm coding. Unless there's active dissension, a team will quickly converge on a common "hand-finished" style. A formatter cannot understand my intentions (I should know, I once wrote one), and it's more important to me that the line breaks and groupings reflect the intention of the code, not just the syntax of the language. (Kevin McGuire freed me from my bondage to automatic code formatters.)

Compact format

The more I can get on a screen, the more I can see without breaking context by scrolling or switching files, which means I can keep less state in my head. Long procedure comments and lots of whitespace made sense for eight-character names and line printers, but now I live in an IDE that does syntax coloring and cross linking. Pixels are my limiting factor, so I want every one to contribute to my understanding of the code. I want the layout to help me understand the code, but no more than that.

A nonprogrammer friend once remarked that code looks like poetry. I get that feeling from really good code—that everything in the text has a purpose, and that it's there to help me understand the idea. Unfortunately, writing code doesn't have the same romantic image as writing poetry.

Code Reviews

Mattias Karlsson

YOU SHOULD DO CODE REVIEWS. Why? Because they *increase code quality* and *reduce defect rate*. But not necessarily for the reasons you might think.

Because they may previously have had some bad experiences with code reviews, many programmers tend to dislike them. I have seen organizations that require that all code pass a formal review before being deployed to production. Often, it is the architect or a lead developer doing this review, a practice that can be described as *architect reviews everything*. This is stated in the company's software development process manual, so the programmers must comply.

There may be some organizations that need such a rigid and formal process, but most do not. In most organizations, such an approach is counterproductive. Reviewees can feel like they are being judged by a parole board. Reviewers need both the time to read the code and the time to keep up to date with all the details of the system; they can rapidly become the bottleneck in this process, and the process soon degenerates.

Instead of simply correcting mistakes in code, the purpose of code reviews should be to *share knowledge* and establish common coding guidelines. Sharing your code with other programmers enables collective code ownership. Let a random team member *walk through the code* with the rest of the team. Instead of looking for errors, you should review the code by trying to learn and understand it.

Be gentle during code reviews. Ensure that comments are *constructive, not caustic*. Introduce different *roles* for the review meeting to avoid having organizational seniority among team members affect the code review. Examples of roles could include having one reviewer focus on documentation, another on exceptions, and a third to look at the functionality. This approach helps to spread the review burden across the team members.

Have a regular *code review day* each week. Spend a couple of hours in a review meeting. Rotate the reviewee every meeting in a simple round-robin pattern. Remember to switch roles among team members every review meeting, too. *Involve newbies* in code reviews. They may be inexperienced, but their fresh university knowledge can provide a different perspective. *Involve experts* for their experience and knowledge. They will identify error-prone code faster and with more accuracy. Code reviews will flow more easily if the team has coding conventions that are checked by tools. That way, code formatting will never be discussed during the code review meeting.

Making code reviews fun is perhaps the most important contributor to success. Reviews are about the people reviewing. If the review meeting is painful or dull, it will be hard to motivate anyone. Make it an *informal code review* whose principal purpose is to share knowledge among team members. Leave sarcastic comments outside, and bring a cake or brown-bag lunch instead.

Coding with Reason

Yechiel Kimchi

TRYING TO REASON about software correctness by hand results in a formal proof that is longer than the code, and more likely to contain errors. Automated tools are preferable but not always possible. What follows describes a middle path: reasoning semiformally about correctness.

The underlying approach is to divide all the code under consideration into short sections—from a single line, such as a function call, to blocks of less than 10 lines—and argue about their correctness. The arguments need only be strong enough to convince your devil's advocate peer programmer.

A section should be chosen so that at each endpoint, the *state of the program* (namely, the program counter and the values of all "living" objects) satisfies an easily described property, and so that the functionality of that section (state transformation) is easy to describe as a single task; these guidelines will make reasoning simpler. Such endpoint properties generalize concepts like *preconditions* and *postconditions* for functions, and *invariants* for loops and classes (with respect to their instances). Striving for sections to be as independent of one another as possible simplifies reasoning and is indispensable when these sections are to be modified.

Many of the coding practices that are well known (although perhaps less well followed) and considered "good" make reasoning easier. Hence, just by *intending* to reason about your code, you already start moving toward a better style and structure. Unsurprisingly, most of these practices can be checked by static code analyzers:

- Avoid using *goto* statements, as they make remote sections highly interdependent.

- Avoid using modifiable global variables, as they make all sections that use them dependent.

- Each variable should have the smallest possible scope. For example, a local object can be declared right before its first usage.

- Make objects *immutable* whenever relevant.

- Make the code readable by using spacing, both horizontal and vertical—e.g., aligning related structures and using an empty line to separate two sections.

- Make the code self-documenting by choosing descriptive (but relatively short) names for objects, types, functions, etc.

- If you need a nested section, make it a function.

- Make your functions short and focused on a single task. The old *24-line limit* still applies. Although screen size and resolution have changed, nothing has changed in human cognition since the 1960s.

- Functions should have few parameters (four is a good upper bound). This does not restrict the data communicated to functions: grouping related parameters into a single object localizes *object invariants*, which simplifies reasoning with respect to their coherence and consistency.

- More generally, each unit of code, from a block to a library, should have a *narrow interface*. Less communication reduces the reasoning required. This means that *getters* that return internal state are a liability—don't ask an object for information to work with. Instead, ask the object to do the work with the information it already has. In other words, *encapsulation is all—and only—about narrow interfaces*.

- In order to preserve class *invariants*, usage of *setters* should be discouraged. Setters tend to allow invariants that govern an object's state to be broken.

As well as reasoning about its correctness, arguing about your code helps you better understand it. Communicate the insights you gain for everyone's benefit.

A Comment on Comments

Cal Evans

IN MY FIRST PROGRAMMING CLASS IN COLLEGE, my teacher handed out two BASIC coding sheets. On the board, the assignment read, "Write a program to input and average 10 bowling scores." Then the teacher left the room. How hard could this be? I don't remember my final solution, but I'm sure it had a FOR/NEXT loop in it and couldn't have been more than 15 lines long in total. Coding sheets—for you kids reading this, yes, we used to write code out longhand before actually entering it into a computer—allowed for around 70 lines of code each. I was very confused as to why the teacher would have given us two sheets. Since my handwriting has always been atrocious, I used the second one to recopy my code very neatly, hoping to get a couple of extra points for style.

Much to my surprise, when I received the assignment back at the start of the next class, I received a barely passing grade. (It was to be an omen to me for the rest of my time in college.) Scrawled across the top of my neatly copied code was "No comments?"

It was not enough that the teacher and I both knew what the program was supposed to do. Part of the point of the assignment was to teach me that my code should explain itself to the next programmer coming behind me. It's a lesson I've not forgotten.

Comments are not evil. They are as necessary to programming as basic branching or looping constructs. Most modern languages have a tool akin to javadoc that will parse properly formatted comments to automatically build an API document. This is a very good start, but not nearly enough. Inside your code should be explanations about what the code is supposed to be doing. Coding by the old adage, "If it was hard to write, it should be hard to read," does a disservice to your client, your employer, your colleagues, and your future self.

On the other hand, you can go too far in your commenting. Make sure that your comments clarify your code but do not obscure it. Sprinkle your code with relevant comments explaining what the code is supposed to accomplish. Your header comments should give any programmer enough information to use your code without having to read it, while your inline comments should assist the next developer in fixing or extending it.

At one job, I disagreed with a design decision made by those above me. Feeling rather snarky, as young programmers often do, I pasted the text of the email instructing me to use their design into the header comment block of the file. It turned out that managers at this particular shop actually reviewed the code when it was committed. It was my first introduction to the term *career-limiting move*.

Comment Only What the Code Cannot Say

Kevlin Henney

THE DIFFERENCE BETWEEN THEORY AND PRACTICE is greater in practice than it is in theory—an observation that certainly applies to comments. In theory, the general idea of commenting code sounds like a worthy one: offer the reader detail, an explanation of what's going on. What could be more helpful than being helpful? In practice, however, comments often become a blight. As with any other form of writing, there is a skill to writing good comments. Much of the skill is in knowing when not to write them.

When code is ill-formed, compilers, interpreters, and other tools will be sure to object. If the code is in some way functionally incorrect, reviews, static analysis, tests, and day-to-day use in a production environment will flush most bugs out. But what about comments? In *The Elements of Programming Style* (Computing McGraw-Hill), Kernighan and Plauger note that "a comment is of zero (or negative) value if it is wrong." And yet such comments often litter and survive in a codebase in a way that coding errors never could. They provide a constant source of distraction and misinformation, a subtle but constant drag on a programmer's thinking.

What of comments that are not technically wrong, but add no value to the code? Such comments are noise. Comments that parrot the code offer nothing extra to the reader—stating something once in code and again in natural language does not make it any truer or more real. Commented-out code is not executable code, so it has no useful effect for either reader or runtime. It also becomes stale very quickly. Version-related comments and commented-out code try to address questions of versioning and history. These questions have already been answered (far more effectively) by version control tools.

A prevalence of noisy comments and incorrect comments in a codebase encourages programmers to ignore all comments, either by skipping past them or by taking active measures to hide them. Programmers are resourceful and will route around anything perceived to be damage: folding comments up; switching coloring scheme so that comments and the background are the same color; scripting to filter out comments. To save a codebase from such misapplications of programmer ingenuity, and to reduce the risk of overlooking any comments of genuine value, comments should be treated as though they were code. Each comment should add some value for the reader, otherwise it is waste that should be removed or rewritten.

What then qualifies as value? Comments should say something code does not and cannot say. A comment explaining what a piece of code should already say is an invitation to change code structure or coding conventions so the code speaks for itself. Instead of compensating for poor method or class names, rename them. Instead of commenting sections in long functions, extract smaller functions whose names capture the former sections' intent. Try to express as much as possible through code. Any shortfall between what you can express in code and what you would like to express in total becomes a plausible candidate for a useful comment. Comment what the code *cannot* say, not simply what it does not say.

Continuous Learning

Clint Shank

WE LIVE IN INTERESTING TIMES. As development gets distributed across the globe, you learn there are lots of people capable of doing your job. You need to keep learning to stay marketable. Otherwise you'll become a dinosaur, stuck in the same job until, one day, you'll no longer be needed or your job gets outsourced to some cheaper resource.

So what do you do about it? Some employers are generous enough to provide training to broaden your skill set. Others may not be able to spare the time or money for any training at all. To play it safe, you need to take responsibility for your own education.

Here's a list of ways to keep you learning. Many of these can be found on the Internet for free:

- Read books, magazines, blogs, Twitter feeds, and websites. If you want to go deeper into a subject, consider joining a mailing list or newsgroup.

- If you really want to get immersed in a technology, get hands on—write some code.

- Always try to work with a mentor, as being the top guy can hinder your education. Although you can learn something from anybody, you can learn a whole lot more from someone smarter or more experienced than you. If you can't find a mentor, consider moving on.

- Use virtual mentors. Find authors and developers on the Web who you really like and read everything they write. Subscribe to their blogs.

- Get to know the frameworks and libraries you use. Knowing how something works makes you know how to use it better. If they're open source, you're really in luck. Use the debugger to step through the code to see what's going on under the hood. You'll get to see code written and reviewed by some really smart people.

- Whenever you make a mistake, fix a bug, or run into a problem, try to really understand what happened. It's likely that someone else ran into the same problem and posted it on the Web. Google is really useful here.

- A good way to learn something is to teach or speak about it. When people are going to listen to you and ask you questions, you'll be highly motivated to learn. Try a lunch-'n'-learn at work, a user group, or a local conference.

- Join or start a study group (à la patterns community) or a local user group for a language, technology, or discipline you are interested in.

- Go to conferences. And if you can't go, many conferences put their talks online for free.

- Long commute? Listen to podcasts.

- Ever run a static analysis tool over the codebase or look at the warnings in your IDE? Understand what they're reporting and why.

- Follow the advice of the Pragmatic Programmers* and learn a new language every year. At least learn a new technology or tool. Branching out gives you new ideas you can use in your current technology stack.

- Not everything you learn has to be about technology. Learn the domain you're working in so you can better understand the requirements and help solve the business problem. Learning how to be more productive—how to work better—is another good option.

- Go back to school.

It would be nice to have the capability that Neo had in *The Matrix*, and simply download the information we need into our brains. But we don't, so it will take a time commitment. You don't have to spend every waking hour learning. A little time—say, each week—is better than nothing. There is (or should be) a life outside of work.

Technology changes fast. Don't get left behind.

* *http://www.pragprog.com/titles/tpp/the-pragmatic-programmer*

Convenience Is
Not an -ility

Gregor Hohpe

MUCH HAS BEEN SAID about the importance and challenges of designing good APIs. It's difficult to get right the first time and it's even more difficult to change later—sort of like raising children. Most experienced programmers have learned that a good API follows a consistent level of abstraction, exhibits consistency and symmetry, and forms the vocabulary for an expressive language. Alas, being aware of the guiding principles does not automatically translate into appropriate behavior. Eating sweets is bad for you.

Instead of preaching from on high, I want to pick on a particular API design "strategy," one that I encounter time and again: the argument of convenience. It typically begins with one of the following "insights":

- I don't want other classes to have to make two separate calls to do this one thing.

- Why should I make another method if it's almost the same as this method? I'll just add a simple `switch`.

- See, it's very easy: if the second string parameter ends with ".txt", the method automatically assumes that the first parameter is a filename, so I really don't need two methods.

While well intended, such arguments are prone to decrease the readability of code using the API. A method invocation like:

```
parser.processNodes(text, false);
```

is virtually meaningless without knowing the implementation or at least consulting the documentation. This method was likely designed for the convenience of the implementer as opposed to the convenience of the caller—"I don't want the caller to have to make two separate calls" translated into "I didn't want to code up two separate methods." There's nothing fundamentally wrong with convenience if it's intended to be the antidote to tediousness, clunkiness, or awkwardness. However, if we think a bit more carefully about it, the antidote to those symptoms is efficiency, consistency, and elegance, not necessarily convenience. APIs are supposed to hide underlying complexity, so we can realistically expect good API design to require some effort. A single large method could certainly be more convenient to write than a well-thought-out set of operations, but would it be easier to use?

The metaphor of API as a language can guide us toward better design decisions in these situations. An API should provide an expressive language, which gives the next layer above sufficient vocabulary to ask and answer useful questions. This does not imply that it should provide exactly one method, or verb, for each question that may be worth asking. A diverse vocabulary allows us to express subtleties in meaning. For example, we prefer to say `run` instead of `walk(true)`, even though it could be viewed as essentially the same operation, just executed at different speeds. A consistent and well-thought-out API vocabulary makes for expressive and easy-to-understand code in the next layer up. More importantly, a composable vocabulary allows other programmers to use the API in ways you may not have anticipated—a great convenience indeed for the users of the API! Next time you are tempted to lump a few things together into one API method, remember that the English language does not have one word for `MakeUpYourRoomBeQuietAndDoYourHomeWork`, even though it would be really convenient for such a frequently requested operation.

Deploy Early
and Often

Steve Berczuk

DEBUGGING THE DEPLOYMENT AND INSTALLATION PROCESSES is often put off until close to the end of a project. In some projects, writing installation tools is delegated to a release engineer who takes on the task as a "necessary evil." Reviews and demonstrations are done from a hand-crafted environment to ensure that everything works. The result is that the team gets no experience with the deployment process or the deployed environment until it may be too late to make changes.

The installation/deployment process is the first thing that the customer sees, and a simple one is the first step to having a reliable (or, at least, easy to debug) production environment. The deployed software is what the customer will use. By not ensuring that the deployment sets up the application correctly, you'll raise questions with your customers before they get to use your software thoroughly.

Starting your project with an installation process will give you time to evolve the process as you move through the product development cycle, and the chance to make changes to the application code to make the installation easier. Running and testing the installation process on a clean environment periodically also provides a check that you have not made assumptions in the code that rely on the development or test environments.

Putting deployment last means that the deployment process may need to be more complicated to work around assumptions in the code. What seemed a great idea in an IDE, where you have full control over an environment, might make for a much more complicated deployment process. It is better to know all the trade-offs sooner rather than later.

While "being able to deploy" doesn't seem to have a lot of business value early on as compared to seeing an application run on a developer's laptop, the simple truth is that until you can demonstrate you application on the target environment, there is a lot of work to do before you can deliver business value. If your rationale for putting off a deployment process is that it is trivial, then do it anyway since it is low cost. If it's too complicated, or if there are too many uncertainties, do what you would do with application code: experiment, evaluate, and refactor the deployment process as you go.

The installation/deployment process is essential to the productivity of your customers or your professional services team, so you should be testing and refactoring this process as you go. We test and refactor the source code throughout a project. The deployment deserves no less.

Distinguish Business Exceptions from Technical

Dan Bergh Johnsson

THERE ARE BASICALLY TWO REASONS that things go wrong at runtime: technical problems that prevent us from using the application and business logic that prevents us from misusing the application. Most modern languages, such as LISP, Java, Smalltalk, and C#, use exceptions to signal both these situations. However, the two situations are so different that they should be carefully held apart. It is a potential source of confusion to represent them both using the same exception hierarchy, not to mention the same exception class.

An unresolvable technical problem can occur when there is a programming error. For example, if you try to access element 83 from an array of size 17, then the program is clearly off track, and some exception should result. The subtler version is calling some library code with inappropriate arguments, causing the same situation on the inside of the library.

It would be a mistake to attempt to resolve these situations you caused yourself. Instead, we let the exception bubble up to the highest architectural level and let some general exception-handling mechanism do what it can to ensure that the system is in a safe state, such as rolling back a transaction, logging and alerting administration, and reporting back (politely) to the user.

A variant of this situation is when *you* are in the "library situation" and a caller has broken the contract of your method, e.g., passing a totally bizarre argument or not having a dependent object set up properly. This is on a par with accessing the 83rd element from 17: the caller should have checked; not doing so is a programmer error on the client side. The proper response is to throw a technical exception.

A different, but still technical, situation is when the program cannot proceed because of a problem in the execution environment, such as an unresponsive database. In this situation, you must assume that the infrastructure did what it could to resolve the issue—repairing connections and retrying a reasonable number of times—and failed. Even if the cause is different, the situation for the calling code is similar: there is little it can do about it. So, we signal the situation through an exception that we let bubble up to the general exception-handling mechanism.

In contrast to these, we have the situation where you cannot complete the call for a domain-logical reason. In this case, we have encountered a situation that is an exception, i.e., unusual and undesirable, but not bizarre or programmatically in error (for example, if I try to withdraw money from an account with insufficient funds). In other words, this kind of situation is a part of the contract, and throwing an exception is just an *alternative return path* that is part of the model and that the client should be aware of and be prepared to handle. For these situations, it is appropriate to create a specific exception or a separate exception hierarchy so that the client can handle the situation on its own terms.

Mixing technical exceptions and business exceptions in the same hierarchy blurs the distinction and confuses the caller about what the method contract is, what conditions it is required to ensure before calling, and what situations it is supposed to handle. Separating the cases gives clarity and increases the chances that technical exceptions will be handled by some application framework, while the business domain exceptions actually are considered and handled by the client code.

Do Lots of Deliberate Practice

Jon Jagger

DELIBERATE PRACTICE IS NOT SIMPLY PERFORMING A TASK. If you ask yourself, "Why am I performing this task?" and your answer is, "To complete the task," then you're not doing deliberate practice.

You do deliberate practice to improve your ability to perform a task. It's about skill and technique. Deliberate practice means repetition. It means performing the task with the aim of increasing your mastery of one or more aspects of the task. It means repeating the repetition. Slowly, over and over again, until you achieve your desired level of mastery. You do deliberate practice to master the task, not to complete the task.

The principal aim of paid development is to finish a product, whereas the principal aim of deliberate practice is to improve your performance. They are not the same. Ask yourself, how much of your time do you spend developing someone else's product? How much developing yourself?

How much deliberate practice does it take to acquire expertise?

- Peter Norvig writes[*] that "it may be that 10,000 hours…is the magic number."

- In *Leading Lean Software Development* (Addison-Wesley Professional), Mary Poppendieck notes that "it takes elite performers a minimum of 10,000 hours of deliberate focused practice to become experts."

---

[*] *http://norvig.com/21-days.html*

The expertise arrives gradually over time—not all at once in the 10,000th hour! Nevertheless, 10,000 hours is a lot: about 20 hours per week for 10 years. Given this level of commitment, you might be worrying that you're just not expert material. You are. Greatness is largely a matter of conscious choice. Your choice. Research over the last two decades has shown that the main factor in acquiring expertise is time spent doing deliberate practice. Innate ability is not the main factor. According to Mary Poppendieck:

> There is broad consensus among researchers of expert performance that inborn talent does not account for much more than a threshold; you have to have a minimum amount of natural ability to get started in a sport or profession. After that, the people who excel are the ones who work the hardest.

There is little point to deliberately practicing something you are already an expert at. Deliberate practice means practicing something you are not good at. Peter Norvig explains:

> The key [to developing expertise] is *deliberative* practice: not just doing it again and again, but challenging yourself with a task that is just beyond your current ability, trying it, analyzing your performance while and after doing it, and correcting any mistakes.

And Mary Poppendieck writes:

> Deliberate practice does not mean doing what you are good at; it means challenging yourself, doing what you are not good at. So it's not necessarily fun.

Deliberate practice is about learning—learning that changes you, learning that changes your behavior. Good luck.

Domain-Specific Languages

Michael Hunger

WHENEVER YOU LISTEN TO A DISCUSSION BY EXPERTS in any domain, be it chess players, kindergarten teachers, or insurance agents, you'll notice that their vocabulary is quite different from everyday language. That's part of what domain-specific languages (DSLs) are about: a specific domain has a specialized vocabulary to describe the things that are particular to that domain.

In the world of software, DSLs are about executable expressions in a language specific to a domain, employing a limited vocabulary and grammar that is readable, understandable, and—hopefully—writable by domain experts. DSLs targeted at software developers or scientists have been around for a long time. The Unix "little languages" found in configuration files and the languages created with the power of LISP macros are some of the older examples.

DSLs are commonly classified as either *internal* or *external*:

Internal DSLs

Are written in a general-purpose programming language whose syntax has been bent to look much more like natural language. This is easier for languages that offer more syntactic sugar and formatting possibilities (e.g., Ruby and Scala) than it is for others that do not (e.g., Java). Most internal DSLs wrap existing APIs, libraries, or business code and provide a wrapper for less mind-bending access to the functionality. They are directly executable by just running them. Depending on the implementation and the domain, they are used to build data structures, define dependencies, run processes or tasks, communicate with other systems, or validate user input. The syntax of an internal DSL is constrained by the host language. There are many patterns—e.g., expression builder, method chaining, and annotation—that can help you to bend the host language to your DSL. If the host language doesn't require recompilation, an internal DSL can be developed quite quickly working side by side with a domain expert.

External DSLs

Are textual or graphical expressions of the language—although textual DSLs tend to be more common than graphical ones. Textual expressions can be processed by a toolchain that includes lexer, parser, model transformer, generators, and any other type of post-processing. External DSLs are mostly read into internal models that form the basis for further processing. It is helpful to define a grammar (e.g., in EBNF). A grammar provides the starting point for generating parts of the toolchain (e.g., editor, visualizer, parser generator). For simple DSLs, a handmade parser may be sufficient—using, for instance, regular expressions. Custom parsers can become unwieldy if too much is asked of them, so it makes sense to look at tools designed specifically for working with language grammars and DSLs—e.g., openArchitectureWare, ANTLR, SableCC, AndroMDA. Defining external DSLs as XML dialects is also quite common, although readability is often an issue—especially for nontechnical readers.

You must always take the target audience of your DSL into account. Are they developers, managers, business customers, or end users? You have to adapt the technical level of the language, the available tools, syntax help (e.g., IntelliSense), early validation, visualization, and representation to the intended audience. By hiding technical details, DSLs can empower users by giving them the ability to adapt systems to their needs without requiring the help of developers. It can also speed up development because of the potential distribution of work after the initial language framework is in place. The language can be evolved gradually. There are also different migration paths for existing expressions and grammars available.

Don't Be Afraid to Break Things

Mike Lewis

EVERYONE WITH INDUSTRY EXPERIENCE has undoubtedly worked on a project where the codebase was precarious at best. The system is poorly factored, and changing one thing always manages to break another unrelated feature. Whenever a module is added, the coder's goal is to change as little as possible, and hold his breath during every release. This is the software equivalent of playing *Jenga* with I-beams in a skyscraper, and is bound for disaster.

The reason that making changes is so nerve-racking is because the system is sick. It needs a doctor, otherwise its condition will only worsen. You already know what is wrong with your system, but you are afraid of breaking the eggs to make your omelet. A skilled surgeon knows that cuts have to be made in order to operate, but she also knows that the cuts are temporary and will heal. The end result of the operation is worth the initial pain, and the patient should heal to a better state than he was in before the surgery.

Don't be afraid of your code. Who cares if something gets temporarily broken while you move things around? A paralyzing fear of change is what got your project into this state to begin with. Investing the time to refactor will pay for itself several times over the lifecycle of your project. An added benefit is that your team's experience dealing with the sick system makes you all experts in knowing how it *should* work. Apply this knowledge rather than resent it. Working on a system you hate is not how anybody should have to spend his time.

Redefine internal interfaces, restructure modules, refactor copy–pasted code, and simplify your design by reducing dependencies. You can significantly reduce code complexity by eliminating corner cases, which often result from improperly coupled features. Slowly transition the old structure into the new one, testing along the way. Trying to accomplish a large refactor in "one big shebang" will cause enough problems to make you consider abandoning the whole effort midway through.

Be the surgeon who isn't afraid to cut out the sick parts to make room for healing. The attitude is contagious and will inspire others to start working on those cleanup projects they've been putting off. Keep a "hygiene" list of tasks that the team feels are worthwhile for the general good of the project. Convince management that even though these tasks may not produce visible results, they will reduce expenses and expedite future releases. Never stop caring about the general "health" of the code.

Don't Be Cute with Your Test Data

Rod Begbie

It was getting late. I was throwing in some placeholder data to test the page layout I'd been working on.

I appropriated the members of The Clash for the names of users. Company names? Song titles by the Sex Pistols would do. Now I needed some stock ticker symbols—just some four-letter words in capital letters.

*I used **those** four-letter words.*

It seemed harmless. Just something to amuse myself, and maybe the other developers the next day before I wired up the real data source.

The following morning, a project manager took some screenshots for a presentation.

PROGRAMMING HISTORY is littered with these kinds of war stories. Things that developers and designers did "that no one else would see," which unexpectedly became visible.

The leak type can vary but, when it happens, it can be deadly to the person, team, or company responsible. Examples include:

- During a status meeting, a client clicks on a button that is as yet unimplemented. He is told, "Don't click that again, you moron."

- A programmer maintaining a legacy system has been told to add an error dialog, and decides to use the output of existing behind-the-scenes logging to power it. Users are suddenly faced with messages such as "Holy database commit failure, Batman!" when something breaks.

- Someone mixes up the test and live administration interfaces, and does some "funny" data entry. Customers spot a $1M "Bill Gates–shaped personal massager" on sale in your online store.

To appropriate the old saying that "a lie can travel halfway around the world while the truth is putting on its shoes," in this day and age, a screw-up can be Dugg, Twittered, and Flibflarbed before anyone in the developer's time zone is awake to do anything about it.

Even your source code isn't necessarily free of scrutiny. In 2004, when a tarball of the Windows 2000 source code made its way onto file-sharing networks, some folks merrily grepped through it for profanity, insults, and other funny content.* (The comment `// TERRIBLE HORRIBLE NO GOOD VERY BAD HACK` has, I will admit, become appropriated by me from time to time since!)

In summary, when writing any text in your code—whether comments, logging, dialogs, or test data—always ask yourself how it will look if it becomes public. It will save some red faces all around.

---

* *http://www.kuro5hin.org/story/2004/2/15/71552/7795*

Don't Ignore
That Error!

Pete Goodliffe

I was walking down the street one evening to meet some friends in a bar. We hadn't shared a beer in some time, and I was looking forward to seeing them again. In my haste, I wasn't looking where I was going. I tripped over the edge of a curb and ended up flat on my face. Well, it serves me right for not paying attention, I guess.

It hurt my leg, but I was in a hurry to meet my friends. So, I pulled myself up and carried on. As I walked farther, the pain was getting worse. Although I'd initially dismissed it as shock, I rapidly realized there was something wrong.

But I hurried on to the bar regardless. I was in agony by the time I arrived. I didn't have a great night out, because I was terribly distracted. In the morning, I went to the doctor and found out I'd fractured my shin bone. Had I stopped when I felt the pain, I would've prevented a lot of extra damage that I caused by walking on it. Probably the worst morning after of my life.

TOO MANY PROGRAMMERS write code like my disastrous night out.

Error, what error? It won't be serious. Honestly. I can ignore it. This is *not* a winning strategy for solid code. In fact, it's just plain laziness. (The wrong sort.) No matter how unlikely you think an error is in your code, you should always check for it, and always handle it. Every time. You're not saving time if you don't; you're storing up potential problems for the future.

We report errors in our code in a number of ways, including:

- **Return codes** can be used as the resulting value of a function to mean "it didn't work." Error return codes are far too easy to ignore. You won't see anything in the code to highlight the problem. Indeed, it's become normal practice to ignore some standard C functions' return values. How often do you check the return value from `printf`?

- **errno** is a curious C aberration, a separate global variable set to signal error. It's easy to ignore, hard to use, and leads to all sorts of nasty problems—for example, what happens when you have multiple threads calling the same function? Some platforms insulate you from pain here; others do not.

- **Exceptions** are a more structured language-supported way of signaling and handling errors. And you can't possibly ignore them. Or can you? I've seen lots of code like this:

```
try {
    // ...do something...
}
catch (...) {} // ignore errors
```

The saving grace of this awful construct is that it highlights the fact that you're doing something morally dubious.

If you ignore an error, turn a blind eye, and pretend that nothing has gone wrong, you run great risks. Just as my leg ended up in a worse state than if I'd stopped walking on it immediately, plowing on regardless of the red flags can lead to very complex failures. Deal with problems at the earliest opportunity. Keep a short account.

Not handling errors leads to:

- **Brittle code.** Code that's filled with exciting, hard-to-find bugs.

- **Insecure code.** Crackers often exploit poor error handling to break into software systems.

- **Poor structure.** If there are errors from your code that are tedious to deal with continually, you probably have a poor interface. Express it so that the errors are less intrusive and their handling is less onerous.

Just as you should check all potential errors in your code, you need to expose all potentially erroneous conditions in your interfaces. Do not hide them, pretending that your services will always work.

Why don't we check for errors? There are a number of common excuses. Which of these do you agree with? How would you counter each one?

- Error handling clutters up the flow of the code, making it harder to read, and harder to spot the "normal" flow of execution.

- It's extra work, and I have a deadline looming.

- I know that this function call will never return an error (printf always works, malloc always returns new memory—if it fails, we have bigger problems...).

- It's only a toy program, and needn't be written to a production-worthy level.

Don't Just Learn the Language, Understand Its Culture

Anders Norås

IN HIGH SCHOOL, I HAD TO LEARN A FOREIGN LANGUAGE. At the time, I thought that I'd get by nicely being good at English, so I chose to sleep through three years of French class. A few years later, I went to Tunisia on vacation. Arabic is the official language there and, being a former French colony, French is also commonly used. English is only spoken in the touristy areas. Because of my linguistic ignorance, I found myself confined at the poolside reading *Finnegans Wake*, James Joyce's tour de force in form and language. Joyce's playful blend of more than 40 languages was a surprising, albeit exhausting, experience. Realizing how interwoven foreign words and phrases gave the author new ways of expressing himself is something I've kept with me in my programming career.

In their seminal book, *The Pragmatic Programmer* (Addison-Wesley Professional), Andy Hunt and Dave Thomas encourage us to learn a new programming language every year. I've tried to live by their advice, and throughout the years, I've had the experience of programming in many languages. My most important lesson from my polyglot adventures is that it takes more than just learning the syntax to learn a language: you need to understand its culture.

You can write Fortran in any language, but to truly learn a language you have to embrace it.

Don't make excuses if your C# code is a long `Main` method with mostly `static` helper methods, but learn why classes make sense. Don't shy away if you have a hard time understanding the lambda expressions used in functional languages—force yourself to use them.

Once you've learned the ropes of a new language, you'll be surprised how you'll start using languages you already know in new ways.

I learned how to use delegates effectively in C# from programming Ruby; releasing the full potential of .NET's generics gave me ideas on how I could make Java generics more useful; and LINQ made it a breeze to teach myself Scala.

You'll also get a better understanding of design patterns by moving between different languages. C programmers find that C# and Java have commoditized the iterator pattern. In Ruby and other dynamic languages, you might still use a visitor, but your implementation won't look like the example from the Gang of Four book.

Some might argue that *Finnegans Wake* is unreadable, while others applaud it for its stylistic beauty. To make the book a less daunting read, single language translations are available. Ironically, the first of these was in French.

Code is in many ways similar. If you write *Wakese* code with a little Python, some Java, and a hint of Erlang, your projects will be a mess. If you instead explore new languages to expand your mind and get fresh ideas on how you can solve things in different ways, you will find that the code you write in your trusty old language gets more beautiful for every new language you've learned.

Don't Nail Your Program into the Upright Position

Verity Stob

I ONCE WROTE A SPOOF C++ QUIZ, in which I satirically suggested the following strategy for exception handling:

> By dint of plentiful try...catch constructs throughout our codebase, we are sometimes able to prevent our applications from aborting. We think of the resultant state as "nailing the corpse in the upright position."

Despite my levity, I was actually summarizing a lesson I received at the knee of Dame Bitter Experience herself.

It was a base application class in our own, homemade C++ library. It had suffered the pokings of many programmers' fingers over the years: nobody's hands were clean. It contained code to deal with all escaped exceptions from everything else. Taking our lead from Yossarian in *Catch-22*, we decided, or rather felt (*decided* implies more thought than went into the construction of this monster) that an instance of this class should live forever or die in the attempt.

To this end, we intertwined multiple exception handlers. We mixed in Windows' structured exception handling with the native kind (remember __try...__except in C++? Me, neither). When things threw unexpectedly, we tried calling them again, pressing the parameters harder. Looking back, I like to think that when writing an inner try...catch handler within the catch clause of another, some sort of awareness crept over me that I might have accidentally taken a slip road from the motorway of good practice into the aromatic but insalubrious lane of lunacy. However, this is probably retrospective wisdom.

Needless to say, whenever something went wrong in applications based on this class, they vanished like Mafia victims at the dockside, leaving behind no useful trail of bubbles to indicate what the hell happened, notwithstanding the dump routines that were supposedly called to record the disaster. Eventually—a long eventually—we took stock of what we had done, and experienced shame. We replaced the whole mess with a minimal and robust reporting mechanism. But this was many crashes down the line.

I wouldn't bother you with this—for surely nobody else could ever be as stupid as we were—but for an online argument I had recently with a bloke whose academic job title declared he should know better. We were discussing Java code in a remote transaction. If the code failed, he argued, it should catch and block the exception *in situ*. ("And then do *what* with it?" I asked. "Cook it for supper?")

He quoted the UI designers' rule: NEVER LET THE USER SEE AN EXCEPTION REPORT, rather as though this settled the matter, what with it being in caps and everything. I wonder if he was responsible for the code in one of those blue-screened ATMs whose photos decorate the feebler blogs, and had been permanently traumatized.

Anyway, if you should meet him, nod and smile and take no notice, as you sidle toward the door.

Don't Rely on "Magic Happens Here"

Alan Griffiths

IF YOU LOOK AT ANY ACTIVITY, process, or discipline from far enough away, it looks simple. Managers with no experience of development think what programmers do is simple, and programmers with no experience of management think the same of what managers do.

Programming is something some people do—some of the time. And the hard part—the thinking—is the least visible and least appreciated by the uninitiated. There have been many attempts to remove the need for this skilled thinking over the decades. One of the earliest and most memorable is the effort by Grace Hopper to make programming languages less cryptic—which some accounts predicted would remove the need for specialist programmers. The result (COBOL) has contributed to the income of many specialist programmers over subsequent decades.

The persistent vision that software development can be simplified by removing programming is, to the programmer who understands what is involved, obviously naïve. But the mental process that leads to this mistake is part of human nature, and programmers are just as prone to making it as everyone else.

On any project, there are likely many things that an individual programmer doesn't get actively involved in: eliciting requirements from users, getting budgets approved, setting up the build server, deploying the application to QA and production environments, migrating the business from the old processes or programs, etc.

When you aren't actively involved in things, there is an unconscious tendency to assume that they are simple and happen "by magic." While the magic continues to happen, all is well. But when—it is usually "when" and not "if"—the magic stops, the project is in trouble.

I've seen projects lose weeks of developer time because no one understood how they relied on "the right" version of a DLL being loaded. When things started failing intermittently, team members looked everywhere else before someone noticed that "a wrong" version of the DLL was being loaded.

Another department was running smoothly—projects delivered on time, no late-night debugging sessions, no emergency fixes. So smoothly, in fact, that senior management decided that things "ran themselves," and it could do without the project manager. Within six months, the projects in the department looked just like the rest of the organization—late, buggy, and continually being patched.

You don't have to understand all the magic that makes your project work, but it doesn't hurt to understand some of it—or to appreciate someone who understands the bits you don't.

Most importantly, make sure that when the magic stops, it can be started again.

Don't Repeat Yourself

Steve Smith

OF ALL THE PRINCIPLES OF PROGRAMMING, Don't Repeat Yourself (DRY) is perhaps one of the most fundamental. The principle was formulated by Andy Hunt and Dave Thomas in *The Pragmatic Programmer*, and underlies many other well-known software development best practices and design patterns. The developer who learns to recognize duplication, and understands how to eliminate it through appropriate practice and proper abstraction, can produce much cleaner code than one who continuously infects the application with unnecessary repetition.

Duplication Is Waste

Every line of code that goes into an application must be maintained, and is a potential source of future bugs. Duplication needlessly bloats the codebase, resulting in more opportunities for bugs and adding accidental complexity to the system. The bloat that duplication adds to the system also makes it more difficult for developers working with the system to fully understand the entire system, or to be certain that changes made in one location do not also need to be made in other places that duplicate the logic they are working on. DRY requires that "every piece of knowledge must have a single, unambiguous, authoritative representation within a system."

Repetition in Process Calls for Automation

Many processes in software development are repetitive and easily automated. The DRY principle applies in these contexts, as well as in the source code of the application. Manual testing is slow, error-prone, and difficult to repeat, so automated test suites should be used where possible. Integrating software can be time consuming and error-prone if done manually, so a build process should be run as frequently as possible, ideally with every check-in. Wherever painful manual processes exist that can be automated, they should be automated and standardized. The goal is to ensure that there is only one way of accomplishing the task, and it is as painless as possible.

Repetition in Logic Calls for Abstraction

Repetition in logic can take many forms. Copy-and-paste *if-then* or *switch-case* logic is among the easiest to detect and correct. Many design patterns have the explicit goal of reducing or eliminating duplication in logic within an application. If an object typically requires several things to happen before it can be used, this can be accomplished with an Abstract Factory or a Factory Method pattern. If an object has many possible variations in its behavior, these behaviors can be injected using the Strategy pattern rather than large *if-then* structures. In fact, the formulation of design patterns themselves is an attempt to reduce the duplication of effort required to solve common problems and discuss such solutions. In addition, DRY can be applied to structures, such as database schema, resulting in normalization.

A Matter of Principle

Other software principles are also related to DRY. The Once and Only Once principle, which applies only to the functional behavior of code, can be thought of as a subset of DRY. The Open/Closed Principle, which states that "software entities should be open for extension, but closed for modification," only works in practice when DRY is followed. Likewise, the well-known Single Responsibility Principle, which requires that a class have "only one reason to change," relies on DRY.

When followed with regard to structure, logic, process, and function, the DRY principle provides fundamental guidance to software developers and aids the creation of simpler, more maintainable, higher-quality applications. While there are scenarios where repetition can be necessary to meet performance or other requirements (e.g., data denormalization in a database), it should be used only where it directly addresses an actual rather than an imagined problem.

Don't Touch
That Code!

Cal Evans

IT HAS HAPPENED TO EVERY ONE OF US AT SOME POINT. Your code was rolled onto the staging server for system testing, and the testing manager writes back that she has hit a problem. Your first reaction is "Quick, let me fix that—I know what's wrong."

In the bigger sense, though, what is wrong is that as a developer you think you should have access to the staging server.

In most web-based development environments, the architecture can be broken down like this:

- Local development and unit testing on the developer's machine

- Development server where manual or automated integration testing is done

- Staging server where the QA team and the users do acceptance testing

- Production server

Yes, there are other servers and services sprinkled in there, like source code control and ticketing, but you get the idea. Using this model, a developer—even a senior developer—should never have access beyond the development server. Most development is done on a developer's local machine using his favorite blend of IDEs, virtual machines, and an appropriate sprinkling of black magic for good luck.

Once checked into SCC, whether automatically or manually, it should be rolled over to the development server, where it can be tested and tweaked if necessary to make sure everything works together. From this point on, though, the developer is a spectator to the process.

The staging manager should package and roll the code to the staging server for the QA team. Just like developers should have no need to access anything beyond the development server, the QA team and the users have no need to touch anything on the development server. If it's ready for acceptance testing, cut a release and roll; don't ask the user to "just look at something real quick" on the development server. Remember, unless you are coding the project by yourself, other people have code there and they may not be ready for the user to see it. The release manager is the only person who should have access to both.

Under no circumstances—ever, at all—should a developer have access to a production server. If there is a problem, your support staff should either fix it or request that you fix it. After it's checked into SCC, they will roll a patch from there. Some of the biggest programming disasters I've been a part of have taken place because someone *cough*me*cough* violated this last rule. If it's broke, production is not the place to fix it.

Encapsulate Behavior, Not Just State

Einar Landre

IN SYSTEMS THEORY, containment is one of the most useful constructs when dealing with large and complex system structures. In the software industry, the value of containment or encapsulation is well understood. Containment is supported by programming language constructs such as subroutines and functions, modules and packages, classes, and so on.

Modules and packages address the larger-scale needs for encapsulation, while classes, subroutines, and functions address the more fine-grained aspects of the matter. Over the years, I have discovered that classes seem to be one of the hardest encapsulation constructs for developers to get right. It's not uncommon to find a class with a single 3,000-line main method, or a class with only set and get methods for its primitive attributes. These examples demonstrate that the developers involved have not fully understood object-oriented thinking, having failed to take advantage of the power of objects as modeling constructs. For developers familiar with the terms POJO (Plain Old Java Object) and POCO (Plain Old C# Object or Plain Old CLR Object), this was the intent in going back to the basics of OO as a modeling paradigm—the objects are plain and simple, but not dumb.

An object encapsulates both state and behavior, where the behavior is defined by the actual state. Consider a door object. It has four states: closed, open, closing, opening. It provides two operations: open and close. Depending on the state, the open and close operations will behave differently. This inherent property of an object makes the design process conceptually simple. It boils down to two simple tasks: allocation and delegation of responsibility to the different objects including the interobject interaction protocols.

How this works in practice is best illustrated with an example. Let's say we have three classes: Customer, Order, and Item. A Customer object is the natural place-holder for the credit limit and credit validation rules. An Order object knows about its associated Customer, and its addItem operation delegates the actual credit check by calling customer.validateCredit(item.price()). If the postcondition for the method fails, an exception can be thrown and the purchase aborted.

Less experienced object-oriented developers might decide to wrap all the business rules into an object very often referred to as OrderManager or OrderService. In these designs, Order, Customer, and Item are treated as little more than record types. All logic is factored out of the classes and tied together in one large, procedural method with a lot of internal *if-then-else* constructs. These methods are easily broken and are almost impossible to maintain. The reason? The encapsulation is broken.

So, in the end, don't break the encapsulation, and use the power of your programming language to maintain it.

Floating-Point Numbers Aren't Real

Chuck Allison

FLOATING-POINT NUMBERS ARE NOT "REAL NUMBERS" in the mathematical sense, even though they are called real in some programming languages, such as Pascal and Fortran. Real numbers have infinite precision and are therefore continuous and nonlossy; floating-point numbers have limited precision, so they are finite, and they resemble "badly behaved" integers, because they're not evenly spaced throughout their range.

To illustrate, assign 2147483647 (the largest signed 32-bit integer) to a 32-bit float variable (x, say), and print it. You'll see 2147483648. Now print x-64. Still 2147483648. Now print x-65, and you'll get 2147483520! Why? Because the spacing between adjacent floats in that range is 128, and floating-point operations round to the nearest floating-point number.

IEEE floating-point numbers are fixed-precision numbers based on base-two scientific notation: $1.d_1 d_2 ... d_{p-1} \times 2^e$, where p is the precision (24 for float, 53 for double). The spacing between two consecutive numbers is 2^{1-p+e}, which can be safely approximated by $\varepsilon|x|$, where ε is the *machine epsilon* (2^{1-p}).

Knowing the spacing in the neighborhood of a floating-point number can help you avoid classic numerical blunders. For example, if you're performing an iterative calculation, such as searching for the root of an equation, there's no sense in asking for greater precision than the number system can give in the neighborhood of the answer. Make sure that the tolerance you request is no smaller than the spacing there, otherwise you'll loop forever.

Since floating-point numbers are approximations of real numbers, there is inevitably a little error present. This error, called *roundoff*, can lead to surprising results.

When you subtract nearly equal numbers, for example, the most significant digits cancel one another out, so what was the least significant digit (where the roundoff error resides) gets promoted to the most significant position in the floating-point result, essentially contaminating any further related computations (a phenomenon known as *smearing*). You need to look closely at your algorithms to prevent such *catastrophic cancellation*. To illustrate, consider solving the equation $x^2 - 100000x + 1 = 0$ with the quadratic formula. Since the operands in the expression $-b + sqrt(b^2 - 4)$ are nearly equal in magnitude, you can instead compute the root $r_1 = -b - sqrt(b^2 - 4)$, and then obtain $r_2 = 1/r_1$, since for any quadratic equation, $ax^2 + bx + c = 0$, the roots satisfy $r_1 r_2 = c/a$.

Smearing can occur in even more subtle ways. Suppose a library naïvely computes e^x by the formula $1 + x + x^2/2 + x^3/3! + \ldots$. This works fine for positive x, but consider what happens when x is a large negative number. The even-powered terms result in large positive numbers, and subtracting the odd-powered magnitudes will not even affect the result. The problem here is that the roundoff in the large, positive terms is in a digit position of much greater significance than the true answer. The answer diverges toward positive infinity! The solution here is also simple: for negative x, compute $e^x = 1/e^{|x|}$.

It should go without saying that you shouldn't use floating-point numbers for financial applications—that's what decimal classes in languages like Python and C# are for. Floating-point numbers are intended for efficient scientific computation. But efficiency is worthless without accuracy, so remember the source of rounding errors, and code accordingly!

Fulfill Your Ambitions with Open Source

Richard Monson-Haefel

CHANCES ARE PRETTY GOOD that you are not developing software at work that fulfills your most ambitious software development daydreams. Perhaps you are developing software for a huge insurance company when you would rather be working at Google, Apple, Microsoft, or your own startup developing the next big thing. You'll never get where you want to go developing software for systems you don't care about.

Fortunately, there is an answer to your problem: open source. There are thousands of open source projects out there, many of them quite active, which offer you any kind of software development experience you could want. If you love the idea of developing operating systems, go help with one of the dozen operating system projects. If you want to work on music software, animation software, cryptography, robotics, PC games, massive online player games, mobile phones, or whatever, you'll almost certainly find at least one open source project dedicated to that interest.

Of course, there is no free lunch. You have to be willing to give up your free time because you probably cannot work on an open source video game at your day job—you still have a responsibility to your employer. In addition, very few people make money contributing to open source projects—some do, but most don't. You should be willing to give up some of your free time (less time playing video games and watching TV won't kill you). The harder you work on an open source project, the faster you'll realize your true ambitions as a programmer. It's also important to consider your employee contract—some employers may restrict what you can contribute, even on your own time. In addition, you need to be careful about violating intellectual property laws having to do with copyright, patents, trademarks, and trade secrets.

Open source provides enormous opportunities for the motivated programmer. First, you get to see how someone else would implement a solution that interests you—you can learn a lot by reading other people's source code. Second, you get to contribute your own code and ideas to the project—not every brilliant idea you have will be accepted, but some might, and you'll learn something new just by working on solutions and contributing code. Third, you'll meet great people with the same passion for the type of software that you have—these open source friendships can last a lifetime. Fourth, assuming you are a competent contributor, you'll be able to add real-world experience in the technology that actually interests you.

Getting started with open source is pretty easy. There is a wealth of documentation out there on the tools you'll need (source code management, editors, programming languages, build systems, etc.). Find the project you want to work on first and learn about the tools that project uses. The documentation on projects themselves will be light in most cases, but this perhaps matters less because the best way to learn is to investigate the code yourself. If you want to get involved, you could offer to help out with the documentation. Or you could start by volunteering to write test code. While that may not sound exciting, the truth is you learn much faster by writing test code for other people's software than almost any other activity in software. Write test code, really good test code. Find bugs, suggest fixes, make friends, work on software you like, and fulfill your software development ambitions.

The Golden Rule
of API Design

Michael Feathers

API DESIGN IS TOUGH, PARTICULARLY IN THE LARGE. If you are designing an API that is going to have hundreds or thousands of users, you have to think about how you might change it in the future and whether your changes might break client code. Beyond that, you have to think about how users of your API affect you. If one of your API classes uses one of its own methods internally, you have to remember that a user could subclass your class and override it, and that could be disastrous. You wouldn't be able to change that method because some of your users have given it a different meaning. Your future internal implementation choices are at the mercy of your users.

API developers solve this problem in various ways, but the easiest way is to lock down the API. If you are working in Java, you might be tempted to make most of your classes and methods `final`. In C#, you might make your classes and methods `sealed`. Regardless of the language you are using, you might be tempted to present your API through a singleton or use `static` factory methods to guard it from people who might override behavior and use your code in ways that may constrain your choices later. This all seems reasonable, but is it really?

Over the past decade, we've gradually realized that unit testing is an extremely important part of practice, but that lesson has not completely permeated the industry. The evidence is all around us. Take an arbitrary untested class that uses a third-party API and try to write unit tests for it. Most of the time, you'll run into trouble. You'll find that the code using the API is stuck to it like glue. There's no way to impersonate the API classes so that you can sense your code's interactions with them, or supply return values for testing.

Over time, this will get better, but only if we start to see testing as a real use case when we design APIs. Unfortunately, it's a little bit more involved than just testing our code. That's where the **Golden Rule of API Design** fits in: *It's not enough to write tests for an API you develop; you have to write unit tests for code that uses your API.* When you follow this rule, you learn firsthand the hurdles that your users will have to overcome when they try to test their code independently.

There is no one way to make it easy for developers to test code that uses your API. `static`, `final`, and `sealed` are not inherently bad constructs. They can be useful at times. But it is important to be aware of the testing issue and, to do that, you have to experience it yourself. Once you have, you can approach it as you would any other design challenge.

The Guru Myth

Ryan Brush

ANYONE WHO HAS WORKED IN SOFTWARE LONG ENOUGH has heard questions like this:

> I'm getting exception *XYZ*. Do you know what the problem is?

Those asking the question rarely bother to include stack traces, error logs, or any context leading to the problem. They seem to think you operate on a different plane, that solutions appear to you without analysis based on evidence. They think you are a guru.

We expect such questions from those unfamiliar with software; to them, systems can seem almost magical. What worries me is seeing this in the software community. Similar questions arise in program design, such as "I'm building inventory management. Should I use optimistic locking?" Ironically, people asking the question are often better equipped to answer it than the question's recipient. The questioners presumably know the context, know the requirements, and can read about the advantages and disadvantages of different strategies. Yet they expect you to give an intelligent answer without context. They expect magic.

It's time for the software industry to dispel this guru myth. "Gurus" are human. They apply logic and systematically analyze problems like the rest of us. They tap into mental shortcuts and intuition. Consider the best programmer you've ever met: at one point, that person knew less about software than you do now. If someone seems like a guru, it's because of years dedicated to learning and refining thought processes. A "guru" is simply a smart person with relentless curiosity.

Of course, there remains a huge variance in natural aptitude. Many hackers out there are smarter, more knowledgeable, and more productive than I may ever be. Even so, debunking the guru myth has a positive impact. For instance, when working with someone smarter than me, I am sure to do the legwork, to provide enough context so that person can efficiently apply his or her skills. Removing the guru myth also means removing a perceived barrier to improvement. Instead of a magical barrier, I see a continuum along which I can advance.

Finally, one of software's biggest obstacles is smart people who purposefully propagate the guru myth. This might be done out of ego, or as a strategy to increase one's value as perceived by a client or employer. Ironically, this attitude can make smart people less valuable, since they don't contribute to the growth of their peers. We don't need gurus. We need experts willing to develop other experts in their field. There is room for all of us.

Hard Work Does Not Pay Off

Olve Maudal

AS A PROGRAMMER, YOU'LL FIND THAT working hard often does not pay off. You might fool yourself and a few colleagues into believing that you are contributing a lot to a project by spending long hours at the office. But the truth is that by working less, you might achieve more—sometimes much more. If you are trying to be focused and "productive" for more than 30 hours a week, you are probably working too hard. You should consider reducing your workload to become more effective and get more done.

This statement may seem counterintuitive and even controversial, but it is a direct consequence of the fact that programming and software development as a whole involve a continuous learning process. As you work on a project, you will understand more of the problem domain and, hopefully, find more effective ways of reaching the goal. To avoid wasted work, you must allow time to observe the effects of what you are doing, reflect on the things that you see, and change your behavior accordingly.

Professional programming is usually not like running hard for a few kilometers, where the goal can be seen at the end of a paved road. Most software projects are more like a long orienteering marathon. In the dark. With only a sketchy map as guidance. If you just set off in one direction, running as fast as you can, you might impress some, but you are not likely to succeed. You need to keep a sustainable pace, and you need to adjust the course when you learn more about where you are and where you are heading.

In addition, you always need to learn more about software development in general and programming techniques in particular. You probably need to read books, go to conferences, communicate with other professionals, experiment with new implementation techniques, and learn about powerful tools that simplify your job. As a professional programmer, you must keep yourself updated in your field of expertise—just as brain surgeons and pilots are expected to keep themselves up to date in their own fields of expertise. You need to spend evenings, weekends, and holidays educating yourself; therefore, you cannot spend your evenings, weekends, and holidays working overtime on your current project. Do you really expect brain surgeons to perform surgery 60 hours a week, or pilots to fly 60 hours a week? Of course not: preparation and education are an essential part of their profession.

Be focused on the project, contribute as much as you can by finding smart solutions, improve your skills, reflect on what you are doing, and adapt your behavior. Avoid embarrassing yourself, and our profession, by behaving like a hamster in a cage spinning the wheel. As a professional programmer, you should know that trying to be focused and "productive" 60 hours a week is not a sensible thing to do. Act like a professional: prepare, effect, observe, reflect, and change.

How to Use a
Bug Tracker

Matt Doar

WHETHER YOU CALL THEM *bugs*, *defects*, or even *design side effects*, there is no getting away from them. Knowing how to submit a good bug report, as well as what to look for in one, are key skills for keeping a project moving along nicely.

A good bug report needs to convey three things:

- How to reproduce the bug, as precisely as possible, and how often this will make the bug appear

- What should have happened, at least in your opinion

- What actually happened, or at least as much information as you have recorded

The amount and quality of information reported in a bug says as much about the reporter as it does about the bug. Angry, terse bugs ("This function sucks!") tell the developers that you were having a bad time, but not much else. A bug with plenty of context to make it easier to reproduce earns the respect of everyone, even if it stops a release.

Bugs are like a conversation, with all the history right there in front of everyone. Don't blame others or deny the bug's very existence. Instead, ask for more information or consider what you could have missed.

Changing the status of a bug—e.g., *Open* to *Closed*—is a public statement of what you think of the bug. Taking the time to explain why you think the bug should be closed will save tedious hours spent later on justifying it to frustrated managers and customers. Changing the priority of a bug is a similar public statement, and just because it's trivial to you doesn't mean it isn't stopping someone else from using the product.

Don't overload a bug's fields for your own purposes. Adding "VITAL:" to the subject field may make it easier for you to sort the results of some report, but it will eventually be copied by others and inevitably mistyped, or will need to be removed for use in some other report. Use a new value or a new field instead, and document how the field is supposed to be used so other people don't have to repeat themselves.

Make sure that everyone knows how to find the bugs that the team is supposed to be working on. This can usually be done using a public query with an obvious name. Make sure everyone is using the same query, and don't update this query without first informing the team that you're changing what everyone is working on.

Finally, remember that a bug is *not* a standard unit of work any more than a line of code is a precise measurement of effort.

Improve Code
by Removing It

Pete Goodliffe

LESS IS MORE. It's a quite trite little maxim, but sometimes it really is true.

One of the improvements I've made to our codebase over the last few weeks is to remove chunks of it.

We'd written the software following XP tenets, including YAGNI (that is, You Aren't Gonna Need It). Human nature being what it is, we inevitably fell short in a few places.

I observed that the product was taking too long to execute certain tasks—simple tasks that should have been near instantaneous. This was because they were overimplemented—festooned with extra bells and whistles that were not required, but at the time had seemed like a good idea.

So I've simplified the code, improved the product performance, and reduced the level of global code entropy simply by removing the offending features from the codebase. Helpfully, my unit tests tell me that I haven't broken anything else during the operation.

A simple and thoroughly satisfying experience.

So why did the unnecessary code end up there in the first place? Why did one programmer feel the need to write extra code, and how did it get past review or the pairing process? Almost certainly something like:

- It was a fun bit of extra stuff, and the programmer wanted to write it. (*Hint: Write code because it adds value, not because it amuses you.*)

- Someone thought that it might be needed in the future, so felt it was best to code it now. (*Hint: That isn't YAGNI. If you don't need it right now, don't write it right now.*)

- It didn't appear to be that big an "extra," so it was easier to implement it rather than go back to the customer to see whether it was really required. (*Hint: It always takes longer to write and to maintain extra code. And the customer is actually quite approachable. A small, extra bit of code snowballs over time into a large piece of work that needs maintenance.*)

- The programmer invented extra requirements that were neither documented nor discussed in order to justify the extra feature. The requirement was actually bogus. (*Hint: Programmers do not set system requirements; the customer does.*)

What are you working on right now? Is it all needed?

Install Me

Marcus Baker

I AM NOT THE SLIGHTEST BIT INTERESTED IN YOUR PROGRAM.

I am surrounded by problems and have a to-do list as long as my arm. The only reason I am at your website right now is because I have heard an unlikely rumor that every one of my problems will be eliminated by your software. You'll forgive me if I'm skeptical.

If eyeball-tracking studies are correct, I've already read the title and I'm scanning for blue underlined text marked *Download now.* As an aside, if I arrived at this page with a Linux browser from a UK IP, chances are I would like the Linux version from a European mirror, so please don't ask. Assuming the file dialog opens straight away, I consign the thing to my download folder and carry on reading.

We all constantly perform cost-benefit analysis of everything we do. If your project drops below my threshold for even a second, I will ditch it and go on to something else. Instant gratification is best.

The first hurdle is *install*. Don't think that's much of a problem? Go to your download folder now and have a look around. Full of *.tar* and *.zip* files, right? What percentage of those have you unpacked? How many have you installed? If you are like me, only a third are doing more than acting as hard drive filler.

I may want doorstep convenience, but I don't want you entering my house uninvited. Before typing **install**, I would like to know exactly where you are putting stuff. It's my computer, and I like to keep it tidy when I can. I also want to be able to remove your program the instant I am disenchanted with it. If I suspect that's impossible, I won't install it in the first place. My machine is stable right now, and I want to keep it that way.

If your program is GUI based, then I want to do something simple and see a result. Wizards don't help, because they do stuff that I don't understand. Chances are, I want to read a file or write one. I don't want to create projects, import directories, or tell you my email address. If all is working, on to the tutorial.

If your software is a library, then I carry on reading your web page looking for a quick start guide. I want the equivalent of "Hello world" in a five-line no-brainer with exactly the output described by your website. No big XML files or templates to fill out, just a single script. Remember, I have also downloaded your rival's framework. You know, the one who always claims to be so much better than yours in the forums? If all is working, on to the tutorial.

There is a tutorial, isn't there? One that talks to me in language I can understand?

And if the tutorial mentions my problem, I'll cheer up. Now that I'm reading about the things I can do, it starts to get interesting, fun even. I'll lean back and sip my tea—did I mention I was from the UK?—and I'll play with your examples and learn to use your creation. If it solves my problem, I'll send you a thank-you email. I'll send you bug reports when it crashes, and suggestions for features, too. I'll even tell all my friends how your software is the best, even though I never did try your rival's. And all because you took such care over my first tentative steps.

How could I ever have doubted you?

Interprocess Communication Affects Application Response Time

Randy Stafford

RESPONSE TIME IS CRITICAL TO SOFTWARE USABILITY. Few things are as frustrating as waiting for some software system to respond, especially when our interaction with the software involves repeated cycles of stimulus and response. We feel as if the software is wasting our time and affecting our productivity. However, the causes of poor response time are less well appreciated, especially in modern applications. Much performance management literature still focuses on data structures and algorithms, issues that can make a difference in some cases but are far less likely to dominate performance in modern multitier enterprise applications.

When performance is a problem in such applications, my experience has been that examining data structures and algorithms isn't the right place to look for improvements. Response time depends most strongly on the number of remote interprocess communications (IPCs) conducted in response to a stimulus. While there can be other local bottlenecks, the number of remote interprocess communications usually dominates. Each remote interprocess communication contributes some nonnegligible latency to the overall response time, and these individual contributions add up, especially when they are incurred in sequence.

A prime example is ripple loading in an application using object-relational mapping. *Ripple loading* describes the sequential execution of many database calls to select the data needed for building a graph of objects (see Lazy Load* in Martin Fowler's *Patterns of Enterprise Application Architecture* [Addison-Wesley Professional]). When the database client is a middle-tier application server rendering a web page, these database calls are usually executed sequentially in a single thread. Their individual latencies accumulate, contributing to the overall response time. Even if each database call takes only 10 milliseconds,

---

* *http://martinfowler.com/eaaCatalog/lazyLoad.html*

a page requiring 1,000 calls (which is not uncommon) will exhibit at least a 10-second response time. Other examples include web-service invocation, HTTP requests from a web browser, distributed object invocation, request–reply messaging, and data-grid interaction over custom network protocols. The more remote IPCs needed to respond to a stimulus, the greater the response time will be.

There are a few relatively obvious and well-known strategies for reducing the number of remote interprocess communications per stimulus. One strategy is to apply the principle of parsimony, optimizing the interface between processes so that exactly the right data for the purpose at hand is exchanged with the minimum amount of interaction. Another strategy is to parallelize the interprocess communications where possible, so that the overall response time becomes driven mainly by the longest-latency IPC. A third strategy is to cache the results of previous IPCs, so that future IPCs may be avoided by hitting local cache instead.

When you're designing an application, be mindful of the number of interprocess communications in response to each stimulus. When analyzing applications that suffer from poor performance, I have often found IPC-to-stimulus ratios of thousands-to-one. Reducing this ratio, whether by caching or parallelizing or some other technique, will pay off much more than changing data structure choice or tweaking a sorting algorithm.

Keep the Build Clean

Johannes Brodwall

HAVE YOU EVER LOOKED AT a list of compiler warnings the length of an essay on bad coding and thought to yourself, "You know, I really should do something about that...but I don't have time just now"? On the other hand, have you ever looked at a lone warning that appeared in a compilation and just fixed it?

When I start a new project from scratch, there are no warnings, no clutter, no problems. But as the codebase grows, if I don't pay attention, the clutter, the cruft, the warnings, and the problems can start piling up. When there's a lot of noise, it's much harder to find the warning that I really want to read among the hundreds of warnings I don't care about.

To make warnings useful again, I try to use a zero-tolerance policy for warnings from the build. Even if the warning isn't important, I deal with it. If it's not critical but still relevant, I fix it. If the compiler warns about a potential null-pointer exception, I fix the cause—even if I "know" the problem will never show up in production. If the embedded documentation (Javadoc or similar) refers to parameters that have been removed or renamed, I clean up the documentation.

If it's something I really don't care about and that really doesn't matter, I ask the team if we can change our warning policy. For example, I find that documenting the parameters and return value of a method in many cases doesn't add any value, so it shouldn't be a warning if they are missing. Or, upgrading to a new version of the programming language may make code that was previously OK now emit warnings. For example, when Java 5 introduced generics, all the old code that didn't specify the generic type parameter would give a warning. This is a sort of warning I don't want to be nagged about (at least, not yet). Having a set of warnings that are out of step with reality does not serve anyone.

By making sure that the build is always clean, I will not have to decide that a warning is irrelevant every time I encounter it. Ignoring things is mental work, and I need to get rid of all the unnecessary mental work I can. Having a clean build also makes it easier for someone else to take over my work. If I leave the warnings, someone else will have to wade through what is relevant and what is not. Or more likely, that person will just ignore all the warnings, including the significant ones.

Warnings from your build are useful. You just need to get rid of the noise to start noticing them. Don't wait for a big cleanup. When something appears that you don't want to see, deal with it right away. You should fix the source of the warning, suppress the warning, or fix the warning policies of your tool. Keeping the build clean is not just about keeping it free of compilation errors or test failures: warnings are also an important and critical part of code hygiene.

Know How to Use Command-Line Tools

Carroll Robinson

TODAY, MANY SOFTWARE DEVELOPMENT TOOLS are packaged in the form of *integrated development environments* (IDEs). Microsoft's Visual Studio and the open source Eclipse are two popular examples, though there are many others. There is a lot to like about IDEs. Not only are they easy to use, but they also relieve the programmer of thinking about a lot of little details involving the build process.

Ease of use, however, has its downside. Typically, when a tool is easy to use, it's because the tool is making decisions for you and doing a lot of things automatically, behind the scenes. Thus, if an IDE is the only programming environment that you ever use, you may never fully understand what your tools are actually doing. You click a button, some magic occurs, and an executable file appears in the project folder.

By working with command-line build tools, you will learn a lot more about what the tools are doing when your project is being built. Writing your own *make* files will help you to understand all of the steps (compiling, assembling, linking, etc.) that go into building an executable file. Experimenting with the many command-line options for these tools is a valuable educational experience as well. To get started with using command-line build tools, you can use open source command-line tools such as GCC, or you can use the ones supplied with your proprietary IDE. After all, a well-designed IDE is just a graphical frontend to a set of command-line tools.

In addition to improving your understanding of the build process, there are some tasks that can be performed more easily or more efficiently with command-line tools than with an IDE. For example, the search and replace capabilities provided by the grep and sed utilities are often more powerful than those found in IDEs. Command-line tools inherently support scripting, which allows for the automation of tasks such as producing scheduled daily builds, creating multiple versions of a project, and running test suites. In an IDE, this kind of automation may be more difficult (if not impossible) to do, as build options are usually specified using GUI dialog boxes and the build process is invoked with a mouse click. If you never step outside of the IDE, you may not even realize that these kinds of automated tasks are possible.

But wait. Doesn't the IDE exist to make development easier and to improve the programmer's productivity? Well, yes. The suggestion presented here is not that you should stop using IDEs. The suggestion is that you should "look under the hood" and understand what your IDE is doing for you. The best way to do that is to learn to use command-line tools. Then, when you go back to using your IDE, you'll have a much better understanding of what it is doing for you and how you can control the build process. On the other hand, once you master the use of command-line tools and experience the power and flexibility that they offer, you may find that you prefer the command line over the IDE.

Know Well More Than Two Programming Languages

Russel Winder

THE PSYCHOLOGY OF PROGRAMMING: people have known for a long time now that programming expertise is related directly to the number of different programming paradigms that a programmer is comfortable with—that is, not that he just knows about or knows a bit of, but that he can genuinely program with.

Every programmer starts with one programming language. That language has a dominating effect on the way that programmer thinks about software. No matter how many years of experience the programmer gets using that language, if she stays with that language, she will know only that language. A one-language programmer is constrained in her thinking by that language.

A programmer who learns a second language will be challenged, especially if that language has a different computational model than the first. C, Pascal, Fortran—all have the same fundamental computational model. Switching from Fortran to C introduces a few, but not many, challenges. Moving from C or Fortran to C++ or Ada introduces fundamental challenges in the way programs behave. Moving from C++ to Haskell is a significant change and hence a significant challenge. Moving from C to Prolog is a very definite challenge.

We can enumerate a number of paradigms of computation: procedural, object-oriented, functional, logic, dataflow, etc. Moving among these paradigms creates the greatest challenges.

Why are these challenges good? That has to do with the way we think about the implementation of algorithms and the idioms and patterns of implementation that apply. In particular, cross-fertilization is at the core of expertise. Idioms for problem solutions that apply in one language may not be possible in another language. Trying to *port* the idioms from one language to another teaches us about both languages and about the problem being solved.

Cross-fertilization in the use of programming languages has huge effects. Perhaps the most obvious is the increased and increasing use of declarative modes of expression in systems implemented in imperative languages. Anyone versed in functional programming can easily apply a declarative approach even when using a language such as C. Using declarative approaches generally leads to shorter and more comprehensible programs. C++, for instance, certainly takes this on board with its wholehearted support for generic programming, which almost necessitates a declarative mode of expression.

The consequence of all this is that it behooves every programmer to be well skilled in programming in at least two different paradigms, and ideally at least the aforementioned five. Programmers should always be interested in learning new languages, preferably from an unfamiliar paradigm. Even if their day job always uses the same programming language, the increased sophistication of use of that language when a person can cross-fertilize from other paradigms should not be underestimated. Employers should take this into account and allow room in their training budget for employees to learn languages that are not currently being used, as a way of increasing the sophistication of the languages that are being used.

Although it's a start, a one-week training course is not sufficient to learn a new language: it generally takes a good few months of use, even if part-time, to gain a proper working knowledge of a language. It is the idioms of use, not just the syntax and computational model, that are the important factors.

Know Your IDE

Heinz Kabutz

IN THE 1980S, our programming environments were typically nothing better than glorified text editors…if we were lucky. Syntax highlighting, which we take for granted nowadays, was a luxury that certainly was not available to everyone. Pretty printers to format our code nicely were usually external tools that had to be run to correct our spacing. Debuggers were also separate programs run to step through our code, but with a lot of cryptic keystrokes.

During the 1990s, companies began to recognize the potential income that they could derive from equipping programmers with better and more useful tools. The Integrated Development Environment (IDE) combined the previous editing features with a compiler, debugger, pretty printer, and other tools. During that time, menus and the mouse also became popular, which meant that developers no longer needed to learn cryptic key combinations to use their editors. They could simply select their command from the menu.

In the 21st century, IDEs have become so commonplace that they are given away for free by companies wishing to gain market share in other areas. The modern IDE is equipped with an amazing array of features. My favorite is automated refactoring, particularly *Extract Method*, where I can select and convert a chunk of code into a method. The refactoring tool will pick up all the parameters that need to be passed into the method, which makes it extremely easy to modify code. My IDE will even detect other chunks of code that could also be replaced by this method and ask me whether I would like to replace them, too.

Another amazing feature of modern IDEs is the ability to enforce style rules within a company. For example, in Java, some programmers have started making all parameters final (which, in my opinion, is a waste of time).

However, since they have such a style rule, all I would need to do to follow it is set it up in my IDE: I would get a warning for any non-final parameter. Style rules can also be used to find probable bugs, such as comparing autoboxed objects for reference equality, e.g., using == on primitive values that are autoboxed into reference objects.

Unfortunately, modern IDEs do not require us to invest effort to learn how to use them. When I first programmed C on Unix, I had to spend quite a bit of time learning how the vi editor worked, due to its steep learning curve. This time spent up front paid off handsomely over the years. I am even typing the draft of this article with vi. Modern IDEs have a very gradual learning curve, which can have the effect that we never progress beyond the most basic usage of the tool.

My first step in learning an IDE is to memorize the keyboard shortcuts. Since my fingers are on the keyboard when I'm typing my code, pressing *Ctrl+Shift+I* to inline a variable prevents breaking the flow, whereas switching to navigate a menu with my mouse interrupts it. These interruptions lead to unnecessary context switches, making me much less productive if I try to do everything the lazy way. The same rule also applies to keyboard skills: learn to touch type; you won't regret the time invested up front.

Lastly, as programmers we have time-proven Unix streaming tools that can help us manipulate our code. For example, if during a code review, I noticed that the programmers had named lots of classes the same, I could find these very easily using the tools find, sed, sort, uniq, and grep, like this:

```
find . -name "*.java" | sed 's/.*\///' | sort | uniq -c | grep -v "^ *1 " | sort -r
```

We expect a plumber coming to our house to be able to use his blowtorch. Let's spend a bit of time to study how to become more effective with our IDE.

Know Your Limits

Greg Colvin

Man's got to know his limitations.
　　　　　　　　　　　　—Dirty Harry

YOUR RESOURCES ARE LIMITED. You only have so much time and money to do your work, including the time and money needed to keep your knowledge, skills, and tools up to date. You can only work so hard, so fast, so smart, and so long. Your tools are only so powerful. Your target machines are only so powerful. So you have to respect the limits of your resources.

How to respect those limits? Know yourself, know your people, know your budgets, and know your stuff. Especially, as a software engineer, know the space and time complexity of your data structures and algorithms, and the architecture and performance characteristics of your systems. Your job is to create an optimal marriage of software and systems.

Space and time complexity are given as the function $O(f(n))$, which for n equal the size of the input is the asymptotic space or time required as n grows to infinity. Important complexity classes for $f(n)$ include $ln(n)$, n, $n\, ln(n)$, n^e, and e^n. As graphing these functions clearly shows, as n gets bigger, $O(ln(n))$ is ever so much smaller than $O(n)$ and $O(n\, ln(n))$, which are ever so much smaller than $O(n^e)$ and $O(e^n)$. As Sean Parent puts it, for achievable n, all complexity classes amount to near-constant, near-linear, or near-infinite.

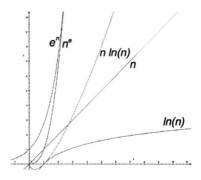

Complexity analysis is measured in terms of an abstract machine, but software runs on real machines. Modern computer systems are organized as hierarchies of physical and virtual machines, including language runtimes, operating systems, CPUs, cache memory, random-access memory, disk drives, and networks. This table shows the limits on random access time and storage capacity for a typical networked server.

	Access time	Capacity
Register	< 1 ns	64 b
Cache line		64 B
L1 cache	1 ns	64 KB
L2 cache	4 ns	8 MB
RAM	20 ns	32 GB
Disk	10 ms	10 TB
LAN	20 ms	> 1 PB
Internet	100 ms	> 1 ZB

Note that capacity and speed vary by several orders of magnitude. Caching and lookahead are used heavily at every level of our systems to hide this variation, but they only work when access is predictable. When cache misses are frequent, the system will be thrashing. For example, to randomly inspect every byte on a hard drive could take 32 years. Even to randomly inspect every byte in RAM could take 11 minutes. Random access is not predictable. What is? That depends on the system, but reaccessing recently used items and accessing items sequentially are usually a win.

Algorithms and data structures vary in how effectively they use caches. For instance:

- Linear search makes good use of lookahead, but requires $O(n)$ comparisons.

- Binary search of a sorted array requires only $O(log(n))$ comparisons.

- Search of a van Emde Boas tree is $O(log(n))$ and cache-oblivious.

How to choose? In the last analysis, by measuring. The table below shows the time required to search arrays of 64-bit integers via these three methods. On my computer:

- Linear search is competitive for small arrays, but loses exponentially for larger arrays.

- van Emde Boas wins hands down, thanks to its predictable access pattern.

	Search time (ns)		
8	50	90	40
64	180	150	70
512	1,200	230	100
4,096	17,000	320	160
	Linear	Binary	vEB

You pays your money and you takes your choice.

—Punch

Know Your Next Commit

Dan Bergh Johnsson

I TAPPED THREE PROGRAMMERS ON THEIR SHOULDERS and asked what they were doing. "I am refactoring these methods," the first answered. "I am adding some parameters to this web action," the second answered. The third answered, "I am working on this user story."

It might seem that the first two were engrossed in the details of their work, while only the third could see the bigger picture, and that he had the better focus. However, when I asked when and what they would commit, the picture changed dramatically. The first two were pretty clear about what files would be involved, and would be finished within an hour or so. The third programmer answered, "Oh, I guess I will be ready within a few days. I will probably add a few classes and might change those services in some way."

The first two did not lack a vision of the overall goal. They had selected tasks they thought led in a productive direction, and could be finished within a couple of hours. Once they had finished those tasks, they would select a new feature or refactoring to work on. All the code written was thus done with a clear purpose and a limited, achievable goal in mind.

The third programmer had not been able to decompose the problem and was working on all aspects at once. He had no idea of what it would take, basically doing speculative programming, hoping to arrive at some point where he would be able to commit. Most probably, the code written at the start of this long session was poorly matched for the solution that came out in the end.

What would the first two programmers do if their tasks took more than two hours? After realizing they had taken on too much, they would most likely throw away their changes, define smaller tasks, and start over. To keep working would have lacked focus and led to speculative code entering the repository. Instead, changes would be thrown away, but the insights kept.

The third programmer might keep on guessing and desperately try to patch together his changes into something that could be committed. After all, you cannot throw away code changes you have done—that would be wasted work, wouldn't it? Unfortunately, not throwing the code away leads to slightly odd code that lacks a clear purpose entering the repository.

At some point, even the commit-focused programmers might fail to find something useful they thought could be finished in two hours. Then, they would go directly into speculative mode, playing around with the code and, of course, throwing away the changes whenever some insight led them back on track. Even these seemingly unstructured hacking sessions have purpose: to learn about the code to be able to define a task that would constitute a productive step.

Know your next commit. If you cannot finish, throw away your changes, then define a new task you believe in with the insights you have gained. Do speculative experimentation whenever needed, but do not let yourself slip into speculative mode without noticing. Do not commit guesswork into your repository.

Large, Interconnected Data Belongs to a Database

Diomidis Spinellis

IF YOUR APPLICATION is going to handle a large, persistent, interconnected set of data elements, don't hesitate to store it in a relational database. In the past, RDBMSs used to be expensive, scarce, complex, and unwieldy beasts. This is no longer the case. Nowadays, RDBMS systems are easy to find—it is likely that the system you're using already has one or two installed. Some very capable RDBMSs, like MySQL and PostgreSQL, are available as open source software, so cost of purchase is no longer an issue. Even better, so-called embedded database systems can be linked as libraries directly into your application, requiring almost no setup or management—two notable open source ones are SQLite and HSQLDB. These systems are extremely efficient.

If your application's data is larger than the system's RAM, an indexed RDBMS table will perform orders of magnitude faster than your library's map collection type, which will thrash virtual memory pages. Modern database offerings can easily grow with your needs. With proper care, you can scale up an embedded database to a larger database system when required. Later on, you can switch from a free, open source offering to a better-supported or more powerful proprietary system.

Once you get the hang of SQL, writing database-centric applications is a joy. After you've stored your properly normalized data in the database, it's easy to extract facts efficiently with a readable SQL query; there's no need to write any complex code. Similarly, a single SQL command can perform complex data changes. For one-off modifications—say, a change in the way you organize your persistent data—you don't even need to write code: just fire up the database's direct SQL interface. This same interface also allows you to experiment with queries, sidestepping a regular programming language's compile–edit cycle.

Another advantage of basing your code around an RDBMS involves the handling of relationships between your data elements. You can describe consistency constraints on your data in a declarative way, avoiding the risk of the dangling pointers you get if you forget to update your data in an edge case. For example, you can specify that if a user is deleted, then the messages sent by that user should be removed as well.

You can also create efficient links between the entities stored in the database any time you want, simply by creating an index. There is no need to perform expensive and extensive refactorings of class fields. In addition, coding around a database allows multiple applications to access your data in a safe way. This makes it easy to upgrade your application for concurrent use and also to code each part of your application using the most appropriate language and platform. For instance, you could write the XML backend of a web-based application in Java, some auditing scripts in Ruby, and a visualization interface in Processing.*

Finally, keep in mind that the RDBMS will sweat hard to optimize your SQL commands, allowing you to concentrate on your application's functionality rather than on algorithmic tuning. Advanced database systems will even take advantage of multicore processors behind your back. And, as technology improves, so will your application's performance.

* *http://www.processing.org/*

Learn Foreign Languages

Klaus Marquardt

PROGRAMMERS NEED TO COMMUNICATE. A lot.

There are periods in a programmer's life when most communication seems to be with the computer—more precisely, with the programs running on that computer. This communication is about expressing ideas in a machine-readable way. This remains an exhilarating prospect: programs are ideas turned into reality, with virtually no physical substance involved.

Programmers need to be fluent in the language of the machine, whether real or virtual, and in the abstractions that can be related to that language via development tools. It is important to learn many different abstractions, otherwise some ideas become incredibly hard to express. Good programmers need to be able to stand outside their daily routine, to be aware of other languages that are expressive for other purposes. The time always comes when this pays off.

Beyond communication with machines, programmers need to communicate with their peers. Today's large projects are more social endeavors than simply the applied art of programming. It is important to understand and express more than the machine-readable abstractions can. Most of the best programmers I know are also very fluent in their mother tongue, and typically in other languages as well. This is not just about communication with others: speaking a language well also leads to a clarity of thought that is indispensable when abstracting a problem. And this is what programming is also about.

Beyond communication with machine, self, and peers, a project has many stakeholders, most with a different or no technical background. They live in testing, quality, and deployment; in marketing and sales; they are end users in some office (or store or home). You need to understand them and their concerns. This is almost impossible if you cannot speak their language—the language of their world, their domain. While you might think a conversation with them went well, they probably didn't.

If you talk to accountants, you need a basic knowledge of cost-center accounting, of tied capital, capital employed, et al. If you talk to marketing or lawyers, some of their jargon and language (and thus, their minds) should be familiar to you. All these domain-specific languages need to be mastered by someone in the project—ideally, the programmers. Programmers are ultimately responsible for bringing the ideas to life via a computer.

And, of course, life is more than software projects. As noted by Charlemagne, *to know another language is to have another soul*. For your contacts beyond the software industry, you will appreciate knowing foreign languages. To know when to listen rather than talk. To know that most language is without words.

Whereof one cannot speak, thereof one must be silent.
—Ludwig Wittgenstein

Learn to Estimate

Giovanni Asproni

AS A PROGRAMMER, you need to be able to provide estimates to your managers, colleagues, and users for the tasks you need to perform, so that they will have a reasonably accurate idea of the time, costs, technology, and other resources needed to achieve their goals.

To be able to estimate well, it is obviously important to learn some estimation techniques. First of all, however, it is fundamental to learn what estimates are, and what they should be used for—as strange as it may seem, many developers and managers don't really know this.

The following exchange between a project manager and a programmer is not atypical:

> *Project Manager:* Can you give me an estimate of the time necessary to develop feature *xyz*?
>
> *Programmer:* One month.
>
> *Project Manager:* That's far too long! We've only got one week.
>
> *Programmer:* I need at least three.
>
> *Project Manager:* I can give you two at most.
>
> *Programmer:* Deal!

The programmer, at the end, comes up with an "estimate" that matches what is acceptable for the manager. But since it is seen to be the programmer's estimate, the manager will hold the programmer accountable to it. To understand what is wrong with this conversation, we need three definitions—estimate, target, and commitment:

- An *estimate* is an approximate calculation or judgment of the value, number, quantity, or extent of something. This definition implies that an estimate is a factual measure based on hard data and previous experience—hopes and wishes must be ignored when calculating it. The definition also implies that, being approximate, an estimate cannot be precise, e.g., a development task cannot be estimated to last 234.14 days.

- A *target* is a statement of a desirable business objective, e.g., "The system must support at least 400 concurrent users."

- A *commitment* is a promise to deliver specified functionality at a certain level of quality by a certain date or event. One example could be "The search functionality will be available in the next release of the product."

Estimates, targets, and commitments are independent from one another, but targets and commitments should be based on sound estimates. As Steve McConnell notes, "The primary purpose of software estimation is not to predict a project's outcome; it is to determine whether a project's targets are realistic enough to allow the project to be controlled to meet them." Thus, the purpose of estimation is to make proper project management and planning possible, allowing the project stakeholders to make commitments based on realistic targets.

What the manager in the preceding conversation was really asking the programmer was to make a commitment based on an unstated target that the manager had in mind, *not* to provide an estimate. The next time you are asked to provide an estimate, make sure everybody involved knows what they are talking about, and your projects will have a better chance of succeeding. Now it's time to learn some techniques....

Learn to Say, "Hello, World"

Thomas Guest

PAUL LEE, username leep, more commonly known as Hoppy, had a reputation as the local expert on programming issues. I needed help. I walked across to Hoppy's desk and asked whether he could take a look at some code for me.

"Sure," said Hoppy, "pull up a chair." I took care not to topple the empty cola cans stacked in a pyramid behind him.

"What code?"

"In a function in a file," I said.

"So, let's take a look at this function." Hoppy moved aside a copy of K&R and slid his keyboard in front of me.

"Where's the IDE?" Apparently, Hoppy had no IDE running, just some editor that I couldn't operate. He grabbed back the keyboard. A few keystrokes later, we had the file open—it was quite a big file—and were looking at the function—it was quite a big function. He paged down to the conditional block I wanted to ask about.

"What would this clause actually do if x is negative?" I asked. "Surely it's wrong."

I'd been trying all morning to find a way to force x to be negative, but the big function in the big file was part of a big project, and the cycle of recompiling and then rerunning my experiments was wearing me down. Couldn't an expert like Hoppy just tell me the answer?

Hoppy admitted he wasn't sure. To my surprise, he didn't reach for K&R. Instead, he copied the code block into a new editor buffer, reindented it, wrapped it up in a function. A short while later, he had coded up a main function that looped forever, prompting the user for input values, passing them to the function, printing out the result. He saved the buffer as a new file, *tryit.c*. All of this I could have done for myself, though perhaps not as quickly. But his next step was wonderfully simple and, at the time, quite foreign to my way of working:

```
$ cc tryit.c && ./a.out
```

Look! His actual program, conceived just a few minutes earlier, was now up and running. We tried a few values and confirmed my suspicions (so I'd been right about something!) and *then* he cross-checked the relevant section of K&R. I thanked Hoppy and left, again taking care not to disturb his cola can pyramid.

Back at my own desk, I closed down my IDE. I'd become so used to working on a big project within a big product that I'd started to think that was what I should be doing. A general-purpose computer can do little tasks, too. I opened a text editor and began typing:

```
#include <stdio.h>
int main()
{
    printf("Hello, World\n");
    return 0;
}
```

Let Your Project Speak for Itself

Daniel Lindner

YOUR PROJECT PROBABLY HAS A VERSION CONTROL SYSTEM IN PLACE.
Perhaps it is connected to a continuous integration server that verifies correctness by automated tests. That's great.

You can include tools for static code analysis in your continuous integration server to gather code metrics. These metrics provide feedback about specific aspects of your code, as well as their evolution over time. When you install code metrics, there will always be a red line that you do not want to cross. Let's assume you started with 20% test coverage and never want to fall below 15%. Continuous integration helps you keep track of all these numbers, but you still have to check regularly. Imagine you could delegate this task to the project itself and rely on it to report when things get worse.

You need to give your project a voice. This can be done by email or instant messaging, informing the developers about the latest decline or improvement in numbers. But it's even more effective to embody the project in your office by using an extreme feedback device (XFD).

The idea of XFDs is to drive a physical device such as a lamp, a portable fountain, a toy robot, or even a USB rocket launcher, based on the results of the automatic analysis. Whenever your limits are broken, the device alters its state. In case of a lamp, it will light up, bright and obvious. You can't miss the message even if you're hurrying out the door to get home.

Depending on the type of extreme feedback device, you can hear the build break, see the red warning signals in your code, or even smell your code smells. The devices can be replicated at different locations if you work on a distributed team. You can place a traffic light in your project manager's office, indicating overall project health state. Your project manager will appreciate it.

Let your creativity guide you in choosing an appropriate device. If your culture is rather geeky, you might look for ways to equip your team mascot with radio-controlled toys. If you want a more professional look, invest in sleek designer lamps. Search the Internet for more inspiration. Anything with a power plug or a remote control has the potential to be used as an extreme feedback device.

The extreme feedback device acts as the voice box of your project. The project now resides physically with the developers, complaining to or praising them according to the rules the team has chosen. You can drive this personification further by applying speech-synthesis software and a pair of loudspeakers. Now your project really speaks for itself.

The Linker Is Not a Magical Program

Walter Bright

DEPRESSINGLY OFTEN (happened to me again just before I wrote this), the view that many programmers have of the process of going from source code to a statically linked executable in a compiled language is:

1. Edit source code.

2. Compile source code into object files.

3. Something magical happens.

4. Run executable.

Step 3 is, of course, the linking step. Why would I say such an outrageous thing? I've been doing tech support for decades, and I get the following concerns again and again:

1. The linker says def is defined more than once.

2. The linker says abc is an unresolved symbol.

3. Why is my executable so large?

Followed by "What do I do now?" usually with the phrases "seems to" and "somehow" mixed in, and an aura of utter bafflement. It's the "seems to" and "somehow" that indicate that the linking process is viewed as a magical process, presumably understandable only by wizards and warlocks. The process of compiling does not elicit these kinds of phrases, implying that programmers generally understand how compilers work, or at least what they do.

A linker is a stupid, pedestrian, straightforward program. All it does is concatenate together the code and data sections of the object files, connect the references to symbols with their definitions, pull unresolved symbols out of the library, and write out an executable. That's it. No spells! No magic! The tedium in writing a linker is typically all about decoding and generating the usually ridiculously over-complicated file formats, but that doesn't change the essential nature of a linker.

So, let's say the linker is saying def is defined more than once. Many programming languages, such as C, C++, and D, have both declarations and definitions. Declarations normally go into header files, like:

```
extern int iii;
```

which generates an external reference to the symbol iii. A definition, on the other hand, actually sets aside storage for the symbol, usually appears in the implementation file, and looks like this:

```
int iii = 3;
```

How many definitions can there be for each symbol? As in the film *Highlander*, there can be only one. So, what if a definition of iii appears in more than one implementation file?

```
// File a.c
int iii = 3;
// File b.c
double iii(int x) { return 3.7; }
```

The linker will complain about iii being multiply defined.

Not only can there be only one, there must be one. If iii appears only as a declaration, but never a definition, the linker will complain about iii being an unresolved symbol.

To determine why an executable is the size it is, take a look at the map file that linkers optionally generate. A map file is nothing more than a list of all the symbols in the executable, along with their addresses. This tells you what modules were linked in from the library, and the sizes of each module. Now you can see where the bloat is coming from. Often, there will be library modules that you have no idea why were linked in. To figure it out, temporarily remove the suspicious module from the library, and relink. The undefined symbol error then generated will indicate who is referencing that module.

Although it is not always immediately obvious why you get a particular linker message, there is nothing magical about linkers. The mechanics are straightforward; it's the details you have to figure out in each case.

The Longevity of Interim Solutions

Klaus Marquardt

WHY DO WE CREATE INTERIM SOLUTIONS?

Typically, there is some immediate problem to solve. It might be internal to the development team, some tooling that fills a gap in the toolchain. It might be external, visible to end users, such as a workaround that addresses missing functionality.

In most systems and teams, you will find some software that is somewhat segregated from the system, that is considered a draft to be changed sometime, that does not follow the standards and guidelines that shaped the rest of the code. Inevitably, you will hear developers complaining about these. The reasons for their creation are many and varied, but the key to an interim solution's success is simple: it is useful.

Interim solutions, however, acquire inertia (or momentum, depending on your point of view). Because they are there, ultimately useful and widely accepted, there is no immediate need to do anything else. Whenever a stakeholder has to decide what action adds the most value, there will be many that are ranked higher than proper integration of an interim solution. Why? Because it is there, it works, and it is accepted. The only perceived downside is that it does not follow the chosen standards and guidelines—except for a few niche markets, this is not considered to be a significant force.

So the interim solution remains in place. Forever.

And if problems arise with that interim solution, it is unlikely that there will be provision for an update that brings it into line with accepted production quality. What to do? A quick interim update on that interim solution often does the job, and will most likely be well received. It exhibits the same strengths as the initial interim solution…it is just more up to date.

Is this a problem?

The answer depends on your project, and on your personal stake in the production code standards. When the system contains too many interim solutions, its entropy or internal complexity grows and its maintainability decreases. However, this is probably the wrong question to ask first. Remember that we are talking about a solution. It may not be your preferred solution—it is unlikely to be anyone's preferred solution—but the motivation to rework this solution is weak.

So what can we do if we see a problem?

1. Avoid creating an interim solution in the first place.

2. Change the forces that influence the decision of the project manager.

3. Leave it as is.

Let's examine these options more closely:

1. Avoidance is simply not an option in many cases. There is an actual problem to solve, and the standards have turned out to be too restrictive. You might spend some energy trying to change the standards—an honorable, albeit tedious, endeavor—and that change will not be effective in time for your problem at hand.

2. The forces are rooted in the project culture, which resists volitional change. It could be successful in very small projects—especially if it's only you—and you just happen to clean the mess without asking in advance. It could also be successful if the project is such a mess that it is visibly stalled, and some time for cleaning up is commonly accepted.

3. The status quo automatically applies if the previous option does not.

You will create many solutions; some of them will be interim, most of them will be useful. The best way to overcome interim solutions is to make them superfluous, to provide a more elegant and useful solution. May you be granted the serenity to accept the things you cannot change, the courage to change the things you can, and the wisdom to know the difference.

Make Interfaces Easy to Use Correctly and Hard to Use Incorrectly

Scott Meyers

ONE OF THE MOST COMMON TASKS in software development is interface specification. Interfaces occur at the highest level of abstraction (user interfaces), at the lowest (function interfaces), and at levels in between (class interfaces, library interfaces, etc.). Regardless of whether you work with end users to specify how they'll interact with a system, collaborate with developers to specify an API, or declare functions private to a class, interface design is an important part of your job. If you do it well, your interfaces will be a pleasure to use and will boost others' productivity. If you do it poorly, your interfaces will be a source of frustration and errors.

Good interfaces are:

Easy to use correctly
> People using a well-designed interface almost always use the interface correctly, because that's the path of least resistance. In a GUI, they almost always click on the right icon, button, or menu entry, because it's the obvious and easy thing to do. In an API, they almost always pass the correct parameters with the correct values, because that's what's most natural. With interfaces that are easy to use correctly, *things just work*.

Hard to use incorrectly
> Good interfaces anticipate mistakes people might make, and make them difficult—ideally, impossible—to commit. A GUI might disable or remove commands that make no sense in the current context, for example, or an API might eliminate argument-ordering problems by allowing parameters to be passed in any order.

97 Things Every Programmer Should Know

A good way to design interfaces that are easy to use correctly is to exercise them before they exist. Mock up a GUI—possibly on a whiteboard or using index cards on a table—and play with it before any underlying code has been created. Write calls to an API before the functions have been declared. Walk through common use cases and specify how you *want* the interface to behave. What do you *want* to be able to click on? What do you *want* to be able to pass? Easy-to-use interfaces seem natural, because they let you do what you want to do. You're more likely to come up with such interfaces if you develop them from a user's point of view. (This perspective is one of the strengths of test-first programming.)

Making interfaces hard to use incorrectly requires two things. First, you must anticipate errors users might make and find ways to prevent them. Second, you must observe how an interface is misused during early release and modify the interface—yes, modify the interface!—to prevent such errors. The best way to prevent incorrect use is to make such use impossible. If users keep wanting to undo an irrevocable action, try to make the action revocable. If they keep passing the wrong value to an API, do your best to modify the API to take the values that users want to pass.

Above all, remember that interfaces exist for the convenience of their users, not their implementers.

Make the Invisible More Visible

Jon Jagger

MANY ASPECTS OF INVISIBILITY are rightly lauded as software principles to uphold. Our terminology is rich in invisibility metaphors—mechanism transparency and information hiding, to name but two. Software and the process of developing it can be, to paraphrase Douglas Adams, *mostly invisible*:

- Source code has no innate presence, no innate behavior, and doesn't obey the laws of physics. It's visible when you load it into an editor, but close the editor and it's gone. Think about it too long and, like the tree falling down with no one to hear it, you start to wonder if it exists at all.

- A running application has presence and behavior, but reveals nothing of the source code it was built from. Google's home page is pleasingly minimal; the goings on behind it are surely substantial.

- If you're 90% done and endlessly stuck trying to debug your way through the last 10%, then you're not 90% done, are you? Fixing bugs is not making progress. You aren't paid to debug. Debugging is waste. It's good to make waste more visible so you can see it for what it is and start thinking about trying not to create it in the first place.

- If your project is apparently on track, and one week later it's six months late, you have problems—the biggest of which is probably not that it's six months late, but the invisibility force fields powerful enough to hide six months of lateness! Lack of visible progress is synonymous with lack of progress.

Invisibility can be dangerous. You think more clearly when you have something concrete to tie your thinking to. You manage things better when you can see them and see them constantly changing:

- Writing unit tests provides evidence about how easy the code unit is to unit test. It helps reveal the presence (or absence) of developmental qualities you'd like the code to exhibit, such as low coupling and high cohesion.

- Running unit tests provides evidence about the code's behavior. It helps reveal the presence (or absence) of runtime qualities you'd like the application to exhibit, such as robustness and correctness.

- Using bulletin boards and cards makes progress visible and concrete. Tasks can be seen as *Not Started*, *In Progress*, or *Done* without reference to a hidden project management tool and without having to chase programmers for fictional status reports.

- Doing incremental development increases the visibility of development progress (or lack of it) by increasing the frequency of development evidence. Completion of releasable software reveals reality; estimates do not.

It's best to develop software with plenty of regular visible evidence. Visibility gives confidence that progress is genuine and not an illusion, deliberate and not unintentional, repeatable and not accidental.

Message Passing Leads to Better Scalability in Parallel Systems

Russel Winder

PROGRAMMERS ARE TAUGHT from the very outset of their study of computing that concurrency—and especially parallelism, a special subset of concurrency—is hard, that only the very best can ever hope to get it right, and even they get it wrong. Invariably, there is great focus on threads, semaphores, monitors, and how hard it is to get concurrent access to variables to be thread-safe.

True, there are many difficult problems, and they can be very hard to solve. But what is the root of the problem? Shared memory. Almost all the problems of concurrency that people go on and on about relate to the use of shared mutable memory: race conditions, deadlock, livelock, etc. The answer seems obvious: either forgo concurrency or eschew shared memory!

Forgoing concurrency is almost certainly not an option. Computers have more and more cores on an almost quarterly basis, so harnessing true parallelism becomes more and more important. We can no longer rely on ever-increasing processor clock speeds to improve application performance. Only by exploiting parallelism will the performance of applications improve. Obviously, not improving performance is an option, but it is unlikely to be acceptable to users.

So can we eschew shared memory? Definitely.

Instead of using threads and shared memory as our programming model, we can use processes and message passing. *Process* here just means a protected independent state with executing code, not necessarily an operating system process. Languages such as Erlang (and occam before it) have shown that processes are a very successful mechanism for programming concurrent and parallel systems. Such systems do not have all the synchronization stresses that shared-memory, multithreaded systems have. Moreover, there is a formal model—Communicating Sequential Processes (CSP)—that can be applied as part of the engineering of such systems.

We can go further and introduce dataflow systems as a way of computing. In a dataflow system, there is no explicitly programmed control flow. Instead, a directed graph of operators, connected by data paths, is set up and then data is fed into the system. Evaluation is controlled by the readiness of data within the system. Definitely no synchronization problems.

That said, languages such as C, C++, Java, Python, and Groovy are the principal languages of systems development, and all of these are presented to programmers as languages for developing shared-memory, multithreaded systems. So what can be done? The answer is to use—or, if they don't exist, create—libraries and frameworks that provide process models and message passing, avoiding all use of shared mutable memory.

All in all, not programming with shared memory, but instead using message passing, is likely to be the most successful way of implementing systems that harness the parallelism that is now endemic in computer hardware. Perhaps bizarrely, although processes predate threads as a unit of concurrency, the future seems to be in using threads to implement processes.

A Message to the Future

Linda Rising

MAYBE IT'S BECAUSE MOST OF THEM ARE SMART PEOPLE, but in all the years I've taught and worked side by side with programmers, it seems that most of them thought that since the problems they were struggling with were difficult, the solutions should be just as difficult for everyone (maybe even for themselves a few months after the code was written) to understand and maintain.

I remember one incident with Joe, a student in my data structures class, who had to come in to show me what he'd written. "Betcha can't guess what it does!" he crowed.

"You're right," I agreed, without spending too much time on his example and wondering how to get an important message across. "I'm sure you've been working hard on this. I wonder, though, if you haven't forgotten something important. Say, Joe, don't you have a younger brother?"

"Yep. Sure do! Phil! He's in your Intro class. He's learning to program, too!" Joe announced proudly.

"That's great," I replied. "I wonder if he could read this code."

"No way!" said Joe. "This is hard stuff!"

"Just suppose," I suggested, "that this was real, working code, and that in a few years, Phil was hired to make a maintenance update. What have you done for him?" Joe just stared at me, blinking. "We know that Phil is really smart, right?"

Joe nodded. "And I hate to say it, but I'm pretty smart, too!" Joe grinned. "So if I can't easily understand what you've done here and your very smart younger brother will likely puzzle over this, what does that mean about what you've written?" Joe looked at his code a little differently, it seemed to me. "How about this," I suggested in my best "I'm your friendly mentor" voice, "Think of every line of code you write as a message for someone in the future—someone who might be your younger brother. Pretend you're explaining to this smart person how to solve this tough problem.

"Is this what you'd like to imagine? That the smart programmer in the future would see your code and say, 'Wow! This is great! I can understand perfectly what's been done here and I'm amazed at what an elegant—no, wait—what a beautiful piece of code this is. I'm going to show the other folks on my team. This is a masterpiece!'

"Joe, do you think you can write code that solves this difficult problem but will be so beautiful it will sing? Yes, just like a haunting melody. I think that anyone who can come up with the very difficult solution you have here could also write something beautiful. Hmm…I wonder if I should start grading on beauty? What do you think, Joe?"

Joe picked up his work and looked at me, a little smile creeping across his face. "I got it, prof, I'm off to make the world better for Phil. Thanks."

Missing Opportunities for Polymorphism

Kirk Pepperdine

POLYMORPHISM IS ONE OF THE GRAND IDEAS that is fundamental to OO. The word, taken from Greek, means many (*poly*) forms (*morph*). In the context of programming, polymorphism refers to many forms of a particular class of objects or method. But polymorphism isn't simply about alternate implementations. Used carefully, polymorphism creates tiny localized execution contexts that let us work without the need for verbose *if-then-else* blocks. Being in a context allows us to do the right thing directly, whereas being outside of that context forces us to reconstruct it so that we can then do the right thing. With careful use of alternate implementations, we can capture context that can help us produce less code that is more readable. This is best demonstrated with some code, such as the following (unrealistically) simple shopping cart:

```
public class ShoppingCart {
    private ArrayList<Item> cart = new ArrayList<Item>();
    public void add(Item item) { cart.add(item); }
    public Item takeNext() { return cart.remove(0);  }
    public boolean isEmpty() { return cart.isEmpty(); }
}
```

Let's say our webshop offers items that can be downloaded and items that need to be shipped. Let's build another object that supports these operations:

```
public class Shipping {
    public boolean ship(Item item, SurfaceAddress address) { ... }
    public boolean ship(Item item, EMailAddress address { ... }
}
```

When a client has completed checkout, we need to ship the goods:

```
while (!cart.isEmpty()) {
    shipping.ship(cart.takeNext(), ???);
}
```

The *???* parameter isn't some new fancy elvis operator; it's asking whether I should email or snail-mail the item. The context needed to answer this question no longer exists. We have could captured the method of shipment in a boolean or enum and then used an *if-then-else* to fill in the missing parameter. Another solution would be to create two classes that both extend Item. Let's call these DownloadableItem and SurfaceItem. Now let's write some code. I'll promote Item to be an interface that supports a single method, ship. To ship the contents of the cart, we will call item.ship(shipper). Classes DownloadableItem and SurfaceItem will both implement ship:

```
public class DownloadableItem implements Item {
    public boolean ship(Shipping shipper, Customer customer) {
        shipper.ship(this, customer.getEmailAddress());
    }
}
public class SurfaceItem implements Item {
    public boolean ship(Shipping shipper, Customer customer) {
        shipper.ship(this, customer.getSurfaceAddress());
    }
}
```

In this example, we've delegated the responsibility of working with Shipping to each Item. Since each item knows how it's best shipped, this arrangement allows us to get on with it without the need for an *if-then-else*. The code also demonstrates a use of two patterns that often play well together: Command and Double Dispatch. Effective use of these patterns relies on careful use of polymorphism. When that happens, there will be a reduction in the number of *if-then-else* blocks in our code.

While there are cases where it's much more practical to use *if-then-else* instead of polymorphism, it is more often the case that a more polymorphic coding style will yield a smaller, more readable and less fragile codebase. The number of missed opportunities is a simple count of the *if-then-else* statements in our code.

News of the Weird: Testers Are Your Friends

Burk Hufnagel

WHETHER THEY CALL THEMSELVES *Quality Assurance* or *Quality Control*, many programmers call them *Trouble*. In my experience, programmers often have an adversarial relationship with the people who test their software. "They're too picky" and "They want everything perfect" are common complaints. Sound familiar?

I'm not sure why, but I've always had a different view of testers. Maybe it's because the "tester" at my first job was the company secretary. Margaret was a very nice lady who kept the office running, and tried to teach a couple of young programmers how to behave professionally in front of customers. She also had a gift for finding any bug, no matter how obscure, in mere moments.

Back then, I was working on a program written by an accountant who thought he was a programmer. Needless to say, it had some serious problems. When I thought I had a piece straightened out, Margaret would try to use it, and, more often than not, it would fail in some new way after just a few keystrokes. It was at times frustrating and embarrassing, but she was such a pleasant person that I never thought to blame her for making me look bad. Eventually, the day came when Margaret was able to cleanly start the program, enter an invoice, print it, and shut it down. I was thrilled. Even better, when we installed it on our customer's machine, it all worked. They never saw any problems because Margaret had helped me find and fix them first.

So that's why I say testers are your friends. You may think the testers make you look bad by reporting trivial issues. But when customers are thrilled because they weren't bothered by all those "little things" that QC made you fix, then you look great. See what I mean?

Imagine this: you're test-driving a utility that uses "groundbreaking artificial intelligence algorithms" to find and fix concurrency problems. You fire it up and immediately notice they misspelled "intelligence" on the splash screen. A little inauspicious, but it's just a typo, right? Then you notice the configuration screen uses checkboxes where there should be radio buttons, and some of the keyboard shortcuts don't work. Now, none of these is a big deal, but as the errors add up, you begin to wonder about the programmers. If they can't get the simple things right, what are the odds that their AI can really find and fix something tricky like concurrency issues?

They could be geniuses who were so focused on making the AI insanely great that they didn't notice those trivial things, and without "picky testers" pointing out the problems, you wound up finding them. And now you're questioning the competency of the programmers.

So, as strange as it may sound, those testers who seem determined to expose every little bug in your code really are your friends.

One Binary

Steve Freeman

I'VE SEEN SEVERAL PROJECTS where the build rewrites some part of the code to generate a custom binary for each target environment. This always makes things more complicated than they should be, and introduces a risk that the team may not have consistent versions on each installation. At a minimum, it involves building multiple, near-identical copies of the software, each of which then has to be deployed to the right place. It means more moving parts than necessary, which means more opportunities to make a mistake.

I once worked on a team where every property change had to be checked in for a full build cycle, so the testers were left waiting whenever they needed a minor adjustment (did I mention that the build took too long as well?). I also worked on a team where the system administrators insisted on rebuilding from scratch for production (using the same scripts that we did), which meant that we had no proof that the version in production was the one that had been through testing. And so on.

The rule is simple: *Build a single binary that you can identify and promote through all the stages in the release pipeline.* Hold environment-specific details *in the environment*. This could mean, for example, keeping them in the component container, in a known file, or in the path.

If your team either has a code-mangling build or stores all the target settings with the code, that suggests that no one has thought through the design carefully enough to separate those features that are core to the application and those that are platform-specific. Or it could be worse: the team knows what to do but can't prioritize the effort to make the change.

Of course, there are exceptions: you might be building for targets that have significantly different resource constraints, but that doesn't apply to the majority of us who are writing "database to screen and back again" applications. Alternatively, you might be living with some legacy mess that's too hard to fix right now. In such cases, you have to move incrementally—but start as soon as possible.

And one more thing: keep the environment information versioned, too. There's nothing worse than breaking an environment configuration and not being able to figure out what changed. The environmental information should be versioned separately from the code, since they'll change at different rates and for different reasons. Some teams use distributed version control systems for this (such as bazaar and git), since they make it easier to push changes made in production environments—as inevitably happens—back to the repository.

Only the Code Tells the Truth

Peter Sommerlad

THE ULTIMATE SEMANTICS OF A PROGRAM is given by the running code. If this is in binary form only, it will be a difficult read! The source code should, however, be available if it is your program, any typical commercial software development, an open source project, or code in a dynamically interpreted language. When you look at the source code, the meaning of the program should be apparent. To know what a program does, the source is ultimately all you can be sure of looking at. Even the most accurate requirements document does not tell the whole truth: it does not contain the detailed story of what the program is actually doing, only the high-level intentions of the requirements analyst. A design document may capture a planned design, but it will lack the necessary detail of the implementation. These documents may have lost sync with the current implementation…or may simply have been lost. Or never written in the first place. The source code may be the only thing left.

With this in mind, ask yourself how clearly your code is telling you or any other programmer what it is doing.

You might say, "Oh, my comments will tell you everything you need to know." But keep in mind that comments are not running code. They can be just as wrong as other forms of documentation. There has been a tradition of saying that comments are unconditionally a good thing, so some programmers unquestioningly write more and more comments, even restating and explaining trivia already obvious in the code. This is the wrong way to clarify your code.

If your code needs comments, consider refactoring it so it doesn't. Lengthy comments can clutter screen space and might even be hidden automatically by your IDE. If you need to explain a change, do so in the version control system check-in message and not in the code.

What can you do to actually make your code tell the truth as clearly as possible? Strive for good names. Structure your code with respect to cohesive functionality, which also eases naming. Decouple your code to achieve orthogonality. Write automated tests explaining the intended behavior and check the interfaces. Refactor mercilessly when you learn how to code a simpler, better solution. Make your code as simple as possible to read and understand.

Treat your code like any other composition, such as a poem, an essay, a public blog, or an important email. Craft what you express carefully, so that it does what it should and communicates as directly as possible what it is doing; so that it still communicates your intention when you are no longer around. Remember that useful code is used much longer than ever intended. Maintenance programmers will thank you. And, if you are a maintenance programmer and the code you are working on does not tell the truth easily, apply the aforementioned guidelines in a proactive manner. Establish some sanity in the code, and keep your own sanity.

Own (and Refactor) the Build

Steve Berczuk

IT IS NOT UNCOMMON for teams that are otherwise highly disciplined about coding practices to neglect build scripts, either out of a belief that they are merely an unimportant detail or from a fear that they are complex and need to be tended to by the cult of release engineering. Unmaintainable build scripts with duplication and errors cause problems of the same magnitude as those in poorly factored code.

One rationale for why disciplined, skilled developers treat the build as something secondary to their work is that build scripts are often written in a different language than source code. Another is that the build is not really "code." These justifications fly in the face of the reality that most software developers enjoy learning new languages, and that the build is what creates executable artifacts for developers and end users to test and run. The code is useless without being built, and the build is what defines the component architecture of the application. The build is an essential part of the development process, and decisions about the build process can make the code and the coding simpler.

Build scripts written using the wrong idioms are difficult to maintain and, more significantly, improve. It is worth spending some time to understand the right way to make a change. Bugs can appear when an application is built with the wrong version of a dependency or when a build-time configuration is wrong.

Traditionally, testing has been something that was always left to the "Quality Assurance" team. We now realize that testing as we code is necessary to being able to deliver value predictably. In much the same way, the build process needs to be owned by the development team.

Understanding the build can simplify the entire development lifecycle and reduce costs. A simple-to-execute build allows a new developer to get started quickly and easily. Automating configuration in the build can enable you to get consistent results when multiple people are working on a project, avoiding an "it works for me" conversation. Many build tools allow you to run reports on code quality, allowing you to sense potential problems early. By spending time understanding how to make the build yours, you can help yourself and everyone else on your team. You can focus on coding features, benefiting your stakeholders and making work more enjoyable.

Learn enough of your build process to know when and how to make changes. Build scripts are code. They are too important to be left to someone else, if for no other reason than because the application is not complete until it is built. The job of programming is not complete until we have delivered working software.

Pair Program and Feel the Flow

Gudny Hauknes, Kari Røssland, and
Ann Katrin Gagnat

IMAGINE THAT YOU ARE TOTALLY ABSORBED by what you are doing—focused, dedicated, and involved. You may have lost track of time. You probably feel happy. You are experiencing flow. It is difficult to both achieve and maintain flow for a whole team of developers since there are so many interruptions, interactions, and other distractions that can easily break it.

If you have already practiced pair programming, you are probably familiar with how pairing contributes to flow. If you have not, we want to use our experiences to motivate you to start right now! To succeed with pair programming, both individual team members and the team as a whole have to put forth some effort.

As a team member, be patient with developers less experienced than you. Confront your fears about being intimidated by more skilled developers. Realize that people are different, and value it. Be aware of your own strengths and weaknesses, as well as those of other team members. You may be surprised by how much you can learn from your colleagues.

As a team, introduce pair programming to promote distribution of skills and knowledge throughout the project. You should solve your tasks in pairs and rotate pairs and tasks frequently. Agree upon a rule of rotation. Put the rule aside or adjust it when necessary. Our experience is that you do not necessarily need to complete a task before rotating it to another pair. Interrupting a task to pass it to another pair may sound counterintuitive, but we have found that it works.

There are numerous situations where flow can be broken, but where pair programming helps you keep it:

- *Reduce the "truck factor."* It's a slightly morbid thought experiment, but how many of your team members would have to be hit by a truck before the team became unable to complete the final deliverable? In other words, how dependent is your delivery on certain team members?

Is knowledge privileged or shared? If you have been rotating tasks among pairs, there is always someone else who has the knowledge and can complete the work. Your team's flow is not as affected by the "truck factor."

- *Solve problems effectively.* If you are pair programming and you run into a challenging problem, you always have someone to discuss it with. Such dialog is more likely to open up possibilities than if you are stuck by yourself. As the work rotates, your solution will be revisited and reconsidered by the next pair, so it does not matter if you did not choose the optimal solution initially.

- *Integrate smoothly.* If your current task involves calling another piece of code, you hope the names of the methods, the docs, and the tests are descriptive enough to give you a grasp of what it does. If not, pairing with a developer who was involved in writing that code will give you better overview and faster integration into your own code. Additionally, you can use the discussion as an opportunity to improve the naming, docs, and testing.

- *Mitigate interruptions.* If someone comes over to ask you a question, or your phone rings, or you have to answer an urgent email, or you have to attend a meeting, your pair programming partner can keep on coding. When you return, your partner is still in the flow and you will quickly catch up and rejoin him.

- *Bring new team members up to speed quickly.* With pair programming, and a suitable rotation of pairs and tasks, newcomers quickly get to know both the code and the other team members.

Flow makes you incredibly productive. But it is also vulnerable. Do what you can to get it, and hold on to it when you've got it!

Prefer Domain-Specific Types to Primitive Types

Einar Landre

ON SEPTEMBER 23, 1999, the $327.6 million Mars Climate Orbiter was lost while entering orbit around Mars due to a software error back on Earth. The error was later called the *metric mix-up*. The ground-station software was working in pounds, while the spacecraft expected newtons, leading the ground station to underestimate the power of the spacecraft's thrusters by a factor of 4.45.

This is one of many examples of software failures that could have been prevented if stronger and more domain-specific typing had been applied. It is also an example of the rationale behind many features in the Ada language, one of whose primary design goals was to implement embedded safety-critical software. Ada has strong typing with static checking for both primitive types and user-defined types:

```
type Velocity_In_Knots is new Float range 0.0 .. 500.00;
type Distance_In_Nautical_Miles is new Float range 0.0 .. 3000.00;
Velocity: Velocity_In_Knots;
Distance: Distance_In_Nautical_Miles;
Some_Number: Float;
Some_Number:= Distance + Velocity; -- Will be caught by the compiler as a type error.
```

Developers in less demanding domains might also benefit from applying more domain-specific typing, where they might otherwise continue to use the primitive data types offered by the language and its libraries, such as strings and floats. In Java, C++, Python, and other modern languages, the abstract data type is known as class. Using classes such as Velocity_In_Knots and Distance_In_Nautical_Miles adds a lot of value with respect to code quality:

- The code becomes more readable, as it expresses concepts of a domain, not just Float or String.

- The code becomes more testable, as the code encapsulates behavior that is easily testable.

- The code facilitates reuse across applications and systems.

The approach is equally valid for users of both statically and dynamically typed languages. The only difference is that developers using statically typed languages get some help from the compiler, while those embracing dynamically typed languages are more likely to rely on their unit tests. The style of checking may be different, but the motivation and style of expression is not.

The moral is to start exploring domain-specific types for the purpose of developing quality software.

Prevent Errors

Giles Colborne

ERROR MESSAGES are the most critical interactions between the user and the rest of the system. They happen when communication between the user and the system is near the breaking point.

It is easy to think of an error as being caused by a wrong input from the user. But people make mistakes in predictable, systematic ways. So it is possible to "debug" the communication between the user and the rest of the system just as you would between other system components.

For instance, say you want the user to enter a date within an allowed range. Rather than letting the user enter any date, it is better to offer a device such as a list or calendar showing only the allowed dates. This eliminates any chance of the user entering a date outside of the range.

Formatting errors are another common problem. For instance, if a user is presented with a *Date* text field and enters an unambiguous date such as "July 29, 2012," it is unreasonable to reject it simply because it is not in a preferred format (such as "DD/MM/YYYY"). It is worse still to reject "29 / 07 / 2012" because it contains extra spaces—this kind of problem is particularly hard for users to understand, as the date appears to be in the desired format.

This error occurs because it is easier to reject the date than parse the three or four most common date formats. These kinds of petty errors lead to user frustration, which in turn lead to additional errors as the user loses concentration. Instead, respect users' preference to enter information, not data.

Another way of avoiding formatting errors is to offer cues—for instance, with a label within the field showing the desired format ("DD/MM/YYYY"). Another cue might be to divide the field into three text boxes of two, two, and four characters.

Cues are different from instructions: cues tend to be hints; instructions are verbose. Cues occur at the point of interaction; instructions appear before the point of interaction. Cues provide context; instructions dictate use.

In general, instructions are ineffective at preventing error. Users tend to assume that interfaces will work in line with their past experience ("Surely everyone knows what 'July 29, 2012' means?"). So instructions go unread. Cues nudge users away from errors.

Another way of avoiding errors is to offer defaults. For instance, users typically enter values that correspond to *today, tomorrow, my birthday, my deadline,* or *the date I entered last time I used this form.* Depending on context, one of these is likely to be a good choice as a smart default.

Whatever the cause, systems should be tolerant of errors. You can facilitate this by providing multiple levels of *undo* to all actions—and, in particular, actions that have the potential to destroy or amend users' data.

Logging and analyzing *undo* actions can also highlight where the interface is drawing users into unconscious errors, such as persistently clicking on the "wrong" button. These errors are often caused by misleading cues or interaction sequences that you can redesign to prevent further error.

Whichever approach you take, most errors are systematic—the result of mis-understandings between the user and the software. Understanding how users think, interpret information, make decisions, and input data will help you debug the interactions between your software and your users.

The Professional Programmer

Robert C. Martin (Uncle Bob)

WHAT IS A PROFESSIONAL PROGRAMMER?

The single most important trait of a professional programmer is *personal responsibility*. Professional programmers take responsibility for their career, their estimates, their schedule commitments, their mistakes, and their workmanship. A professional programmer does not pass that responsibility off on others.

- *If you are a professional, then you are responsible for your own career.* You are responsible for reading and learning. You are responsible for staying up to date with the industry and the technology. Too many programmers feel that it is their employer's job to train them. Sorry, this is just dead wrong. Do you think doctors behave that way? Do you think lawyers behave that way? No, they train themselves on their own time, and their own nickel. They spend much of their off-hours reading journals and decisions. They keep themselves up to date. And so must we. The relationship between you and your employer is spelled out nicely in your employment contract. In short: your employer promises to pay you, and you promise to do a good job.

- *Professionals take responsibility for the code they write.* They do not release code unless they *know* it works. Think about that for a minute. How can you possibly consider yourself a professional if you are willing to release code that you are not sure of? Professional programmers expect QA to find *nothing* because *they don't release their code until they've thoroughly tested it.* Of course, QA will find some problems, because no one is perfect. But as professionals, our *attitude* must be that we will leave nothing for QA to find.

- *Professionals are team players.* They take responsibility for the output of the whole team, not just their own work. They help one another, teach one another, learn from one another, and even cover for one another when necessary. When one teammate falls down, the others step in, knowing that one day they'll be the ones to need cover.

- *Professionals do not tolerate big bug lists.* A huge bug list is sloppy. Systems with thousands of issues in the issue-tracking database are tragedies of carelessness. Indeed, in most projects, the very need for an issue-tracking system is a symptom of carelessness. Only the very biggest systems should have bug lists so long that automation is required to manage them.

- *Professionals do not make a mess.* They take pride in their workmanship. They keep their code clean, well structured, and easy to read. They follow agreed-upon standards and best practices. They never, *ever* rush. Imagine that you are having an out-of-body experience watching a doctor perform open-heart surgery on *you*. This doctor has a *deadline* (in the literal sense). He must finish before the heart-lung bypass machine damages too many of your blood cells. How do you want him to behave? Do you want him to behave like the typical software developer, rushing and making a mess? Do you want him to say, "I'll go back and fix this later"? Or do you want him to hold carefully to his disciplines, taking his time, confident that his approach is the best approach he can reasonably take. Do you want a mess, or professionalism?

Professionals are responsible. They take responsibility for their own careers. They take responsibility for making sure their code works properly. They take responsibility for the quality of their workmanship. They do not abandon their principles when deadlines loom. Indeed, when the pressure mounts, professionals hold ever tighter to the disciplines they know are right.

Put Everything Under Version Control

Diomidis Spinellis

PUT EVERYTHING IN ALL YOUR PROJECTS UNDER VERSION CONTROL. The resources you need are there: free tools like Subversion, Git, Mercurial, and CVS; plentiful disk space; cheap and powerful servers; ubiquitous networking; and even project-hosting services. After you've installed the version control software, all you need in order to put your work in its repository is to issue the appropriate command in a clean directory containing your code. And there are just two new basic operations to learn: you *commit* your code changes to the repository and you *update* your working version of the project with the repository's version.

Once your project is under version control, you can obviously track its history, see who wrote what code, and refer to a file or project version through a unique identifier. More importantly, you can make bold code changes without fear—no more commented-out code just in case you need it in the future, because the old version lives safely in the repository. You can (and should) *tag* a software release with a symbolic name so that you can easily revisit in the future the exact version of the software your customer runs. You can create *branches* of parallel development: most projects have an active development branch and one or more maintenance branches for released versions that are actively supported.

A version control system minimizes friction among developers. When programmers work on independent software parts, these get integrated almost by magic. When they step on one another's toes, the system notices and allows them to sort out the conflicts. With some additional setup, the system can notify all developers for each committed change, establishing a common understanding of the project's progress.

When you set up your project, don't be stingy: place *all* the project's assets under version control. In addition to the source code, include the documentation, tools, build scripts, test cases, artwork, and even libraries. With the complete project safely tucked into the (regularly backed up) repository, the potential damage of losing your disk or data is minimized. Setting up for development on a new machine involves simply checking out the project from the repository. This simplifies distributing, building, and testing the code on different platforms: on each machine, a single update command will ensure that the software is the current version.

Once you've seen the beauty of working with a version control system, following a couple of rules will make you and your team even more effective:

- Commit each logical change in a separate operation. Lumping many changes together in a single commit will make it difficult to disentangle them in the feature. This is especially important when you make project-wide refactorings or style changes, which can easily obscure other modifications.

- Accompany each commit with an explanatory message. At a minimum, describe succinctly what you've changed, but if you also want to record the change's rationale, this is the best place to store it.

- Finally, avoid committing code that will break a project's build, otherwise you'll become unpopular with the project's other developers.

Life under a version control system is too good to ruin it with easily avoidable missteps.

Put the Mouse Down and Step Away from the Keyboard

Burk Hufnagel

YOU'VE BEEN FOCUSED FOR HOURS on some gnarly problem, and there's no solution in sight. So you get up to stretch your legs or to hit the vending machines and, on the way back, the answer suddenly becomes obvious.

Does this scenario sound familiar? Ever wonder why it happens? The trick is that while you're coding, the logical part of your brain is active and the creative side is shut out. It can't present anything to you until the logical side takes a break.

Here's a real-life example: I was cleaning up some legacy code and ran into an "interesting" method. It was designed to verify that a string contained a valid time using the format *hh:mm:ss xx*, where *hh* represents the hour, *mm* represents minutes, *ss* represents seconds, and *xx* is either *AM* or *PM*.

The method used the following code to convert two characters (representing the hour) into a number, and verify it was within the proper range:

```
try {
    Integer.parseInt(time.substring(0, 2));
} catch (Exception x) {
    return false;
}
if (Integer.parseInt(time.substring(0, 2)) > 12) {
    return false;
}
```

The same code appeared twice more, with appropriate changes to the character offset and upper limit, to test the minutes and seconds. The method ended with these lines to check for *AM* and *PM*:

```
if (!time.substring(9, 11).equals("AM") &
    !time.substring(9, 11).equals("PM")) {
    return false;
}
```

If none of this series of comparisons failed, returning false, the method returned true.

If the preceding code seems wordy and difficult to follow, don't worry. I thought so, too—which meant I'd found something worth cleaning up. I refactored it and wrote a few unit tests, just to make sure it still worked.

When I finished, I felt pleased with the results. The new version was easy to read, half the size, and more accurate because the original code tested only the upper boundary for the hours, minutes, and seconds.

While getting ready for work the next day, an idea popped in my head: why not validate the string using a regular expression? After a few minutes of typing, I had a working implementation in just one line of code. Here it is:

```
public static boolean validateTime(String time) {
    return time.matches("(0[1-9]|1[0-2]):[0-5][0-9]:[0-5][0-9] ([AP]M)");
}
```

The point of this story is not that I eventually replaced over 30 lines of code with just one. The point is that until I got away from the computer, I thought my first attempt was the best solution to the problem.

So, the next time you hit a nasty problem, do yourself a favor. Once you really understand the problem, go do something involving the creative side of your brain—sketch out the problem, listen to some music, or just take a walk outside. Sometimes the best thing you can do to solve a problem is to put the mouse down and step away from the keyboard.

Read Code

Karianne Berg

WE PROGRAMMERS ARE WEIRD CREATURES. We love writing code. But when it comes to reading it, we usually shy away. After all, writing code is so much more fun, and reading code is hard—sometimes almost impossible. Reading other people's code is particularly hard. Not necessarily because other people's code is bad, but because they probably think and solve problems in a different way than you. But did you ever consider that reading someone else's code could improve your own?

The next time you read some code, stop and think for a moment. Is the code easy or hard to read? If it is hard to read, why is that? Is the formatting poor? Is naming inconsistent or illogical? Are several concerns mixed together in the same piece of code? Perhaps the choice of language prohibits the code from being readable. Try to learn from other people's mistakes, so that your code won't contain the same ones. You may receive a few surprises. For example, dependency-breaking techniques may be good for low coupling, but they can sometimes also make code harder to read. And what some people call *elegant code*, others call *unreadable*.

If the code is easy to read, stop to see if there is something useful you can learn from it. Maybe there's a design pattern in use that you don't know about, or had previously struggled to implement. Perhaps the methods are shorter and their names more expressive than yours. Some open source projects are full of good examples of how to write brilliant, readable code—while others serve as examples of the exact opposite! Check out some of their code and take a look.

Reading your own old code, from a project you are not currently working on, can also be an enlightening experience. Start with some of your oldest code and work your way forward to the present. You will probably find that it is not at all as easy to read as when you wrote it. Your early code may also have a certain embarrassing entertainment value, kind of in the same way as being reminded of all the things you said when you were drinking in the pub last night. Look at how you have developed your skills over the years—it can be truly motivating. Observe what areas of the code are hard to read, and consider whether you are still writing code in the same way today.

So, the next time you feel the need to improve your programming skills, don't read another book. Read code.

Read the Humanities

Keith Braithwaite

IN ALL BUT THE SMALLEST DEVELOPMENT PROJECT, people work with people. In all but the most abstracted field of research, people write software for people to support them in some goal of theirs. People write software with people for people. It's a people business. Unfortunately, what is taught to programmers too often equips them very poorly to deal with people they work for and with. Luckily, there is an entire field of study that can help.

For example, Ludwig Wittgenstein makes a very good case in *Philosophical Investigations* (Wiley-Blackwell), and elsewhere, that any language we use to speak to one another is not—cannot be—a serialization format for getting a thought or idea or picture out of one person's head and into another's. Already, we should be on our guard against misunderstanding when we "gather requirements." Wittgenstein also shows that our ability to understand one another at all does not arise from shared definitions, it arises from a shared experience, from a form of life. This may be one reason why programmers who are steeped in their problem domain tend to do better than those who stand apart from it.

Lakoff and Johnson present us with a catalog of *Metaphors We Live By* (University of Chicago Press), suggesting that language is largely metaphorical, and that these metaphors offer an insight into how we understand the world. Even seemingly concrete terms like *cash flow*, which we might encounter in talking about a financial system, can be seen as metaphorical: "money is a fluid." How does that metaphor influence the way we think about systems that handle money? Or we might talk about layers in a stack of protocols, with some high level and some low level. This is powerfully metaphorical: the user is "up" and the technology is "down." This exposes our thinking about the structure of the systems we build. It can also mark a lazy habit of thought that we might benefit from breaking from time to time.

Martin Heidegger studied closely the ways that people experience tools. Programmers build and use tools, we think about and create and modify and recreate tools. Tools are objects of interest to us. But for its users, as Heiddeger shows in *Being and Time* (Harper Perennial), a tool becomes an invisible thing understood only in use. For users, tools only become objects of interest when they don't work. This difference in emphasis is worth bearing in mind whenever usability is under discussion.

Eleanor Rosch overturned the Aristotelean model of the categories by which we organize our understanding of the world. When programmers ask users about their desires for a system, we tend to ask for definitions built out of predicates. This is very convenient for us. The terms in the predicates can very easily become attributes on a class or columns in a table. These sorts of categories are crisp, disjoint, and tidy. Unfortunately, as Rosch showed in "Natural Categories"[*] and later works, that just isn't how people in general understand the world. They understand it in ways that are based on examples. Some examples, so-called prototypes, are better than others and so the resulting categories are fuzzy, they overlap, they can have rich internal structure. Insofar as we insist on Aristotelean answers, we can't ask users the right questions about the user's world, and will struggle to come to the common understanding we need.

* *Cognitive Psychology* 4: 328–50 (1973)

Reinvent the Wheel Often

Jason P. Sage

Just use something that exists—it's silly to reinvent the wheel....

HAVE YOU EVER HEARD THIS OR SOME VARIATION THEREOF? Sure you have! Every developer and student probably hears comments like this frequently. Why, though? Why is reinventing the wheel so frowned upon? Because, more often than not, existing code is working code. It has already gone through some sort of quality control and rigorous testing, and is being used successfully. Additionally, the time and effort invested in reinvention are unlikely to pay off as well as using an existing product or codebase. Should you bother reinventing the wheel? Why? When?

Perhaps you have seen publications about patterns in software development, or books on software design. These books can be sleepers, regardless of how wonderful the information contained in them is. The same way that watching a movie about sailing is very different from going sailing, so too is using existing code versus designing your own software from the ground up, testing it, breaking it, repairing it, and improving it along the way.

Reinventing the wheel is not just an exercise in where to place code constructs: it is about how to get an intimate knowledge of the inner workings of various components that already exist. Do you know how memory managers work? Virtual paging? Could you implement these yourself? How about double-linked lists? Dynamic array classes? ODBC clients? Could you write a graphical user interface that works like a popular one you know and like? Can you create your own web-browser widgets? Do you know when to write a multiplexed system versus a multithreaded one? How to decide between a file- or a memory-based database?

Most developers simply have never created these types of core software implementations themselves and therefore do not have an intimate knowledge of how they work. The consequence is that all these kinds of software are viewed as mysterious black boxes that just work. Understanding only the surface of the water is not enough to reveal the hidden dangers beneath. Not knowing the deeper things in software development will limit your ability to create stellar work.

Reinventing the wheel and getting it wrong is more valuable than nailing it first time. There are lessons learned from trial and error that have an emotional component to them that reading a technical book alone just cannot deliver!

Learned facts and book smarts are crucial, but becoming a great programmer is as much about acquiring experience as it is about collecting facts. Reinventing the wheel is as important to a developer's education and skill as weightlifting is to a body builder.

Resist the Temptation of the Singleton Pattern

Sam Saariste

THE SINGLETON PATTERN SOLVES MANY OF YOUR PROBLEMS. You know that you only need a single instance. You have a guarantee that this instance is initialized before it's used. It keeps your design simple by having a global access point. It's all good. What's not to like about this classic design pattern?

Quite a lot, it turns out. Tempting they may be, but experience shows that most singletons really do more harm than good. They hinder testability and harm maintainability. Unfortunately, this additional wisdom is not as widespread as it should be, and singletons continue to be irresistible to many programmers. But they are worth resisting:

- *The single-instance requirement is often imagined.* In many cases, it's pure speculation that no additional instances will be needed in the future. Broadcasting such speculative properties across an application's design is bound to cause pain at some point. Requirements will change. Good design embraces this. Singletons don't.

- *Singletons cause implicit dependencies between conceptually independent units of code.* This is problematic both because they are hidden and because they introduce unnecessary coupling between units. This code smell becomes pungent when you try to write unit tests, which depend on loose coupling and the ability to selectively substitute a mock implementation for a real one. Singletons prevent such straightforward mocking.

- *Singletons also carry implicit persistent state, which again hinders unit testing.* Unit testing depends on tests being independent of one another, so the tests can be run in any order and the program can be set to a known state before the execution of every unit test. Once you have introduced singletons with mutable state, this may be hard to achieve. In addition, such globally accessible persistent state makes it harder to reason about the code, especially in a multithreaded environment.

- *Multithreading introduces further pitfalls to the singleton pattern.* As straightforward locking on access is not very efficient, the so-called double-checked locking pattern (DCLP) has gained in popularity. Unfortunately, this may be a further form of fatal attraction. It turns out that in many languages, DCLP is not thread-safe and, even where it is, there are still opportunities to get it subtly wrong.

The cleanup of singletons may present a final challenge:

- *There is no support for explicitly killing singletons.* This can be a serious issue in some contexts—for example, in a plug-in architecture where a plug-in can only be safely unloaded after all its objects have been cleaned up.

- *There is no order to the implicit cleanup of singletons at program exit.* This can be troublesome for applications that contain singletons with interdependencies. When shutting down such applications, one singleton may access another that has already been destroyed.

Some of these shortcomings can be overcome by introducing additional mechanisms. However, this comes at the cost of additional complexity in code that could have been avoided by choosing an alternative design.

Therefore, restrict your use of the Singleton pattern to the classes that truly must never be instantiated more than once. Don't use a singleton's global access point from arbitrary code. Instead, direct access to the singleton should come from only a few well-defined places, from where it can be passed around via its interface to other code. This other code is unaware, and so does not depend on whether a singleton or any other kind of class implements the interface. This breaks the dependencies that prevented unit testing and improves the maintainability. So, the next time you are thinking about implementing or accessing a singleton, I hope you'll pause and think again.

The Road to Performance
Is Littered with Dirty
Code Bombs

Kirk Pepperdine

MORE OFTEN THAN NOT, performance tuning a system requires you to alter code. When we need to alter code, every chunk that is overly complex or highly coupled is a dirty code bomb lying in wait to derail the effort. The first casualty of dirty code will be your schedule. If the way forward is smooth, it will be easy to predict when you'll finish. Unexpected encounters with dirty code will make it very difficult to make a sane prediction.

Consider the case where you find an execution hot spot. The normal course of action is to reduce the strength of the underlying algorithm. Let's say you respond to your manager's request for an estimate with an answer of 3–4 hours. As you apply the fix, you quickly realize that you've broken a dependent part. Since closely related things are often necessarily coupled, this breakage is most likely expected and accounted for. But what happens if fixing that dependency results in other dependent parts breaking? Furthermore, the farther away the dependency is from the origin, the less likely you are to recognize it as such and account for it in your estimate. All of a sudden, your 3–4-hour estimate can easily balloon to 3–4 weeks. Often, this unexpected inflation in the schedule happens one or two days at a time. It is not uncommon to see "quick" refactorings eventually taking several months to complete. In these instances, the damage to the credibility and political capital of the responsible team will range from severe to terminal. If only we had a tool to help us identify and measure this risk....

In fact, we have many ways of measuring and controlling the degree and depth of coupling and complexity of our code. Software metrics can be used to count the occurrences of specific features in our code. The values of these counts do correlate with code quality. Two of a number of metrics that measure coupling are fan-in and fan-out. Consider fan-out for classes: it is defined as the number of classes referenced either directly or indirectly from a class of interest. You can think of this as a count of all the classes that must be compiled before your class can be compiled. Fan-in, on the other hand, is a count of all classes that depend upon the class of interest. Knowing fan-out and fan-in, we can calculate an instability factor using $I = fo / (fi + fo)$. As I approaches 0, the package becomes more stable. As I approaches 1, the package becomes unstable. Packages that are stable are low-risk targets for recoding, whereas unstable packages are more likely to be filled with dirty code bombs. The goal in refactoring is to move I closer to 0.

When using metrics, one must remember that they are only rules of thumb. Based purely on math, we can see that increasing fi without changing fo will move I closer to 0. There is, however, a downside to a very large fan-in value: these classes will be more difficult to alter without breaking dependents. Also, without addressing fan-out, you're not really reducing your risks, so some balance must be applied.

One downside to software metrics is that the huge array of numbers that metrics tools produce can be intimidating to the uninitiated. That said, software metrics can be a powerful tool in our fight for clean code. They can help us to identify and eliminate dirty code bombs before they are a serious risk to a performance-tuning exercise.

Simplicity Comes from Reduction

Paul W. Homer

"DO IT AGAIN...," my boss told me as his finger pressed hard on the Delete key. I watched the computer screen with an all-too-familiar sinking feeling, as my code—line after line—disappeared into oblivion.

My boss, Stefan, wasn't always the most vocal of people, but he knew bad code when he saw it. And he knew exactly what to do with it.

I had arrived in my present position as a student programmer with lots of energy and plenty of enthusiasm but absolutely no idea how to code. I had this horrible tendency to think that the solution to every problem was to add in another variable some place. Or throw in another line. On a bad day, instead of the logic getting better with each revision, my code gradually got larger, more complex, and further away from working consistently.

It's natural, particularly when you're in a rush, to just want to make the most minimal changes to an existing block of code, even if it is awful. Most programmers will preserve bad code, fearing that starting anew will require significantly more effort than just going back to the beginning. That can be true for code that is close to working, but there is just some code that is beyond all help.

More time gets wasted in trying to salvage bad work than it should. Once something becomes a resource sink, it needs to be discarded. Quickly.

Not that one should easily toss away all of that typing, naming, and formatting. My boss's reaction was extreme, but it did force me to rethink the code on the second (or occasionally third) attempt. Still, the best approach to fixing bad code is to flip into a mode where the code is mercilessly refactored, shifted around, or deleted.

The code should be simple. There should be a minimal number of variables, functions, declarations, and other syntactic language necessities. Extra lines, extra variables…extra *anything*, really, should be purged immediately. What's there, what's left, should be just enough to get the job done, completing the algorithm or performing the calculations. Anything and everything else is just extra, unwanted noise, introduced accidentally, obscuring the flow, and hiding the important stuff.

Of course, if that doesn't do it, then just delete it all and type it in over again. Drawing from one's memory in that way can often help cut through a lot of unnecessarily clutter.

The Single Responsibility Principle

Robert C. Martin (Uncle Bob)

ONE OF THE MOST FOUNDATIONAL PRINCIPLES OF GOOD DESIGN IS:

> Gather together those things that change for the same reason, and separate those
> things that change for different reasons.

This principle is often known as the *single responsibility principle*, or SRP. In
short, it says that a subsystem, module, class, or even a function, should not
have more than one reason to change. The classic example is a class that has
methods that deal with business rules, reports, and databases:

```
public class Employee {
    public Money calculatePay() ...
    public String reportHours() ...
    public void save() ...
}
```

Some programmers might think that putting these three functions together
in the same class is perfectly appropriate. After all, classes are supposed to
be collections of functions that operate on common variables. However, the
problem is that the three functions change for entirely different reasons. The
calculatePay function will change whenever the business rules for calculating
pay do. The reportHours function will change whenever someone wants a different format for the report. The save function will change whenever the DBAs
change the database schema. These three reasons to change combine to make
Employee very volatile. It will change for *any* of those reasons. More importantly,
any classes that depend upon Employee will be affected by those changes.

Good system design means that we separate the system into components that
can be independently deployed. Independent deployment means that if we
change one component, we do not have to redeploy any of the others. However,
if Employee is used heavily by many other classes in other components, then every
change to Employee is likely to cause the other components to be redeployed,

thus negating a major benefit of component design (or SOA, if you prefer the trendier name). The following simple partitioning resolves the issues:

```
public class Employee {
    public Money calculatePay() ...
}
public class EmployeeReporter {
    public String reportHours(Employee e) ...
}
public class EmployeeRepository {
    public void save(Employee e) ...
}
```

Each class can be placed in a component of its own. Or rather, all the reporting classes can go into the reporting component. All the database-related classes can go into the repository component. And all the business rules can go into the business rule component.

The astute reader will see that there are still dependencies in the above solution. That Employee is still depended upon by the other classes. So if Employee is modified, the other classes will likely have to be recompiled and redeployed. Thus, Employee cannot be modified and then independently deployed. However, the other classes can be modified and independently deployed. No modification of one of them can force any of the others to be recompiled or redeployed. Even Employee could be independently deployed through a careful use of the *dependency inversion principle* (DIP), but that's a topic for a different book.*

Careful application of the SRP, separating things that change for different reasons, is one of the keys to creating designs that have an independently deployable component structure.

---

* *http://www.amazon.com/dp/0135974445/*

Start from Yes

Alex Miller

RECENTLY, I WAS AT A GROCERY STORE, searching high and low for "edam-ame" (which I only vaguely knew was some kind of a vegetable). I wasn't sure whether this was something I'd find in the vegetable section, the frozen section, or in a can. I gave up and tracked down an employee to help me out. She didn't know, either!

The employee could have responded in many different ways. She could have made me feel ignorant for not knowing where to look, or given me vague possibilities, or even just told me they didn't have the item. But instead, she treated the request as an opportunity to find a solution and help a customer. She called other employees and within minutes had guided me to the exact item, nestled in the frozen section.

The employee in this case looked at a request and started from the premise that we would solve the problem and satisfy the request. She started from *yes* instead of starting from *no*.

When I was first placed in a technical leadership role, I felt that my job was to protect my beautiful software from the ridiculous stream of demands coming from product managers and business analysts. I started most conversations seeing a request as something to defeat, not something to grant.

At some point, I had an epiphany that maybe there was a different way to work that merely involved shifting my perspective from starting at *no* to starting at *yes*. In fact, I've come to believe that starting from *yes* is actually an essential part of being a technical leader.

This simple change radically altered how I approached my job. As it turns out, there are a lot of ways to say *yes*. When someone says to you, "Hey, this app would really be the bee's knees if we made all the windows round and translucent!", you could reject it as ridiculous. But it's frequently better to start with "Why?" instead. Often, there is some actual and compelling reason why that person is asking for round, translucent windows in the first place. For example, you may be just about to sign a big, new customer with a standards committee that mandates round, translucent windows.

Usually, you'll find that when you know the context of the request, new possibilities open up. It's common for the request to be accomplished with the existing product in some other way, allowing you to say *yes* with no work at all: "Actually, in the user preferences, you can download the round, translucent windows skin and turn it on."

Sometimes the other person will simply have an idea that you find incompatible with your view of the product. I find it's usually helpful to turn that "Why?" on yourself. Sometimes the act of voicing the reason will make it clear that your first reaction doesn't make sense. If not, you might need to kick it up a notch and bring in other key decision makers. Remember, the goal of all of this is to say *yes* to the other person and try to make it work, not just for him but for you and your team as well.

If you can voice a compelling explanation as to why the feature request is incompatible with the existing product, then you are likely to have a productive conversation about whether you are building the right product. Regardless of how that conversation concludes, everyone will focus more sharply on what the product is, and what it is not.

Starting from *yes* means working with your colleagues, not against them.

Step Back and Automate, Automate, Automate

Cay Horstmann

I WORKED WITH PROGRAMMERS WHO, when asked to produce a count of the lines of code in a module, pasted the files into a word processor and used its "line count" feature. And they did it again next week. And the week after. It was bad.

I worked on a project that had a cumbersome deployment process, involving code signing and moving the result to a server, requiring many mouse clicks. Someone automated it, and the script ran hundreds of times during final testing, far more often than anticipated. It was good.

So, why do people do the same task over and over instead of stepping back and taking the time to automate it?

Common misconception #1: Automation is only for testing
Sure, test automation is great, but why stop there? Repetitive tasks abound in any project: version control, compiling, building JAR files, documentation generation, deployment, and reporting. For many of these tasks, the script is mightier than the mouse. Executing tedious tasks becomes faster and more reliable.

Common misconception #2: I have an IDE, so I don't have to automate
Did you ever have a "But it (checks out/builds/passes tests) on my machine?" argument with your teammates? Modern IDEs have thousands of potential settings, and it is essentially impossible to ensure that all team members have identical configurations. Build automation systems such as Ant or Autotools give you control and repeatability.

Common misconception #3: I need to learn exotic tools in order to automate
You can go a long way with a decent shell language (such as bash or Power-Shell) and a build automation system. If you need to interact with websites, use a tool such as iMacros or Selenium.

Common misconception #4: I can't automate this task because I can't deal with these file formats
If a part of your process requires Word documents, spreadsheets, or images, it may indeed be challenging to automate it. But is that really necessary? Can you use plain text? Comma-separated values? XML? A tool that generates a drawing from a text file? Often, a slight tweak in the process can yield good results with a dramatic reduction in tediousness.

Common misconception #5: I don't have the time to figure it out
You don't have to learn all of bash or Ant to get started. Learn as you go. When you have a task that you think can and should be automated, learn just enough about your tools to do it. And do it early in a project when time is usually easier to find. Once you have been successful, you (and your boss) will see that it makes sense to invest in automation.

Take Advantage of Code Analysis Tools

Sarah Mount

THE VALUE OF TESTING is something that is drummed into software developers from the early stages of their programming journey. In recent years, the rise of unit testing, test-driven development, and agile methods has attested to a surge of interest in making the most of testing throughout all phases of the development cycle. However, testing is just one of many tools that you can use to improve the quality of code.

Back in the mists of time, when C was still a new phenomenon, CPU time and storage of any kind were at a premium. The first C compilers were mindful of this and so cut down on the number of passes through the code they made by removing some semantic analyses. This meant that the compiler checked for only a small subset of the bugs that could be detected at compile time. To compensate, Stephen Johnson wrote a tool called *lint*—which removes the fluff from your code—that implemented some of the static analyses that had been removed from its sister C compiler. Static analysis tools, however, gained a reputation for giving large numbers of false-positive warnings and warnings about stylistic conventions that aren't always necessary to follow.

The current landscape of languages, compilers, and static analysis tools is very different. Memory and CPU time are now relatively cheap, so compilers can afford to check for more errors. Almost every language boasts at least one tool that checks for violations of style guides, common gotchas, and sometimes cunning errors that can be hard to catch, such as potential null pointer dereferences.

The more sophisticated tools, such as Splint for C or Pylint for Python, are configurable, meaning that you can choose which errors and warnings the tool emits with a configuration file, via command-line switches, or in your IDE. Splint will even let you annotate your code in comments to give it better hints about how your program works.

If all else fails, and you find yourself looking for simple bugs or standards violations that are not caught by your compiler, IDE, or lint tools, then you can always roll your own static checker. This is not as difficult as it might sound. Most languages, particularly ones branded *dynamic*, expose their abstract syntax tree and compiler tools as part of their standard library. It is well worth getting to know the dusty corners of standard libraries that are used by the development team of the language you are using, as these often contain hidden gems that are useful for static analysis and dynamic testing. For example, the Python standard library contains a disassembler which tells you the bytecode used to generate some compiled code or code object. This sounds like an obscure tool for compiler writers on the python-dev team, but it is actually surprisingly useful in everyday situations. One thing this library can disassemble is your last stack trace, giving you feedback on exactly which bytecode instruction threw the last uncaught exception.

So, don't let testing be the end of your quality assurance—take advantage of analysis tools, and don't be afraid to roll your own.

Test for Required Behavior, Not Incidental Behavior

Kevlin Henney

A COMMON PITFALL IN TESTING is to assume that exactly what an implementation does is precisely what you want to test for. At first glance, this sounds more like a virtue than a pitfall. Phrased another way, however, the issue becomes more obvious: a common pitfall in testing is to hardwire tests to the specifics of an implementation, where those specifics are incidental and have no bearing on the desired functionality.

When tests are hardwired to implementation incidentals, changes to the implementation that are actually compatible with the required behavior may cause tests to fail, leading to false positives. Programmers typically respond either by rewriting the test or by rewriting the code. Assuming that a false positive is actually a true positive is often a consequence of fear, uncertainty, or doubt. It has the effect of raising the status of incidental behavior to required behavior. In rewriting a test, programmers either refocus the test on the required behavior (good) or simply hardwire it to the new implementation (not good). Tests need to be sufficiently precise, but they also need to be accurate.

For example, in a three-way comparison, such as Java's String.compareTo or C's strcmp, the requirements on the result are that it is negative if the lefthand side is less than the right, positive if the lefthand side is greater than the right, and zero if they are considered equal. This style of comparison is used in many APIs, including the comparator for C's qsort function and compareTo in Java's Comparable interface. Although the specific values –1 and +1 are commonly used in implementations to signify *less than* and *greater than*, respectively, programmers often mistakenly assume that these values represent the actual requirement and consequently write tests that nail this assumption up in public.

A similar issue arises with tests that assert spacing, precise wording, and other aspects of textual formatting and presentation that are incidental. Unless you are writing, for example, an XML generator that offers configurable formatting, spacing should not be significant to the outcome. Likewise, hardwiring placement of buttons and labels on UI controls reduces the option to change and refine these incidentals in the future. Minor changes in implementation and inconsequential changes in formatting suddenly become build breakers.

Overspecified tests are often a problem with whitebox approaches to unit testing. Whitebox tests use the structure of the code to determine the test cases needed. The typical failure mode of whitebox testing is that the tests end up asserting that the code does what the code does. Simply restating what is already obvious from the code adds no value and leads to a false sense of progress and security.

To be effective, tests need to state contractual obligations rather than parrot implementations. They need to take a blackbox view of the units under test, sketching out the interface contracts in executable form. Therefore, align tested behavior with required behavior.

Test Precisely
and Concretely

Kevlin Henney

IT IS IMPORTANT TO TEST for the desired, essential behavior of a unit of code, rather than for the incidental behavior of its particular implementation. But this should not be taken or mistaken as an excuse for vague tests. Tests need to be both accurate *and* precise.

Something of a tried, tested, and testing classic, sorting routines offer an illustrative example. Implementing a sorting algorithm is not necessarily an everyday task for a programmer, but sorting is such a familiar idea that most people believe they know what to expect from it. This casual familiarity, however, can make it harder to see past certain assumptions.

When programmers are asked, "What would you test for?", by far and away the most common response is something like, "The result of sorting is a sorted sequence of elements." While this is true, it is not the whole truth. When prompted for a more precise condition, many programmers add that the resulting sequence should be the same length as the original. Although correct, this is still not enough. For example, given the following sequence:

    3 1 4 1 5 9

The following sequence satisfies a postcondition of being sorted in nondescending order and having the same length as the original sequence:

    3 3 3 3 3 3

Although it satisfies the spec, it is also most certainly not what was meant! This example is based on an error taken from real production code (fortunately caught before it was released), where a simple slip of a keystroke or a momentary lapse of reason led to an elaborate mechanism for populating the whole result with the first element of the given array.

The full postcondition is that the result is sorted *and* that it holds a permutation of the original values. This appropriately constrains the required behavior.

That the result length is the same as the input length comes out in the wash and doesn't need restating.

Even stating the postcondition in the way described is not enough to give you a good test. A good test should be readable. It should be comprehensible and simple enough that you can see readily that it is correct (or not). Unless you already have code lying around for checking that a sequence is sorted and that one sequence contains a permutation of values in another, it is quite likely that the test code will be more complex than the code under test. As Tony Hoare observed:

> There are two ways of constructing a software design: one way is to make it so simple that there are *obviously* no deficiencies and the other is to make it so complicated that there are no *obvious* deficiencies.

Using concrete examples eliminates this accidental complexity and opportunity for accident. For example, given the following sequence:

```
3 1 4 1 5 9
```

The result of sorting is the following:

```
1 1 3 4 5 9
```

No other answer will do. Accept no substitutes.

Concrete examples help to illustrate general behavior in an accessible and unambiguous way. The result of adding an item to an empty collection is not simply that it is not empty: it is that the collection now has a single item, and that the single item held is the item added. Two or more items would qualify as not empty, and would also be wrong. A single item of a different value would also be wrong. The result of adding a row to a table is not simply that the table is one row bigger; it's also that the row's key can be used to recover the row added. And so on.

In specifying behavior, tests should not simply be accurate: they must also be precise.

Test While You Sleep (and over Weekends)

Rajith Attapattu

RELAX. I am not referring to offshore development centers, overtime on weekends, or working the night shift. Rather, I want to draw your attention to how much computing power we have at our disposal. Specifically, how much we are not harnessing to make our lives as programmers a little easier. Are you constantly finding it difficult to get enough computing power during the work day? If so, what are your test servers doing outside of normal work hours? More often than not, the test servers are idling overnight and over the weekend. You can use this to your advantage.

- *Have you been guilty of committing a change without running all the tests?* One of the main reasons programmers don't run test suites before committing code is because of the length of time they may take. When deadlines are looming and push comes to shove, humans naturally start cutting corners. One way to address this is to break down your large test suite into two or more profiles. A smaller, mandatory test profile that is quick to run will help to ensure that tests are run before each commit. All of the test profiles (including the mandatory profile—just to be sure) can be automated to run overnight, ready to report their results in the morning.

- *Have you had enough opportunity to test the stability of your product?* Longer-running tests are vital for identifying memory leaks and other stability issues. They are seldom run during the day, as it will tie up time and resources. You could automate a soak test to be run during the night, and a bit longer over the weekend. From 6:00 PM Friday to 6:00 AM the following Monday, there are 60 hours' worth of potential testing time.

- *Are you getting quality time on your performance testing environment?* I have seen teams bickering with each other to get time on the performance testing environment. In most cases, neither team gets enough quality time during the day, while the environment is virtually idle after hours. The servers and the network are not as busy during the night or over the weekend. It's an ideal time to run some quality performance tests.

- *Are there too many permutations to test manually?* In many cases, your product is targeted to run on a variety of platforms. For example, both 32-bit and 64-bit, on Linux, Solaris, and Windows, or simply on different versions of the same operating system. To make matters worse, many modern applications expose themselves to a plethora of transport mechanisms and protocols (HTTP, AMQP, SOAP, CORBA, etc.). Manually testing all of these permutations is very time consuming and most likely done close to a release due to resource pressure. Alas, it may be too late in the cycle to catch certain nasty bugs.

Automated tests run during the night or over weekends will ensure that all these permutations are tested more often. With a little bit of thinking and some scripting knowledge, you can schedule a few *cron* jobs to kick off some testing at night and over the weekend. There are also many testing tools out there that could help. Some organizations even have server grids that pool servers across different departments and teams to ensure that resources are utilized efficiently. If this is available in your organization, you can submit tests to be run at night or over weekends.

Testing Is the Engineering Rigor of Software Development

Neal Ford

DEVELOPERS LOVE TO USE TORTURED METAPHORS when trying to explain what it is they do to family members, spouses, and other nontechies. We frequently resort to bridge building and other "hard" engineering disciplines. All these metaphors fall down quickly, though, when you start trying to push them too hard. It turns out that software development is *not* like many of the "hard" engineering disciplines in lots of important ways.

Compared to "hard" engineering, the software development world is at about the same place the bridge builders were when the common strategy was to build a bridge and then roll something heavy over it. If it stayed up, it was a good bridge. If not, well, time to go back to the drawing board. Over the past few thousand years, engineers have developed mathematics and physics they can use for a structural solution without having to build it to see what it does. We don't have anything like that in software, and perhaps never will because software is in fact very different. For a deep-dive exploration of the comparison between software "engineering" and regular engineering, "What is Software Design?", written by Jack Reeves in *C++ Journal* in 1992, is a classic.* Even though it was written almost two decades ago, it is still remarkably accurate. Reeves painted a gloomy picture in this comparison, but the thing that was missing in 1992 was a strong testing ethos for software.

* *http://www.developerdotstar.com/mag/articles/reeves_design.html*

Testing "hard" things is tough because you have to build them to test them, which discourages speculative building just to see what will happen. But the building process in software is ridiculously cheap. We've developed an entire ecosystem of tools that make it easy to do just that: unit testing, mock objects, test harnesses, and lots of other stuff. Other engineers would love to be able to build something and test it under realistic conditions. As software developers, we should embrace testing as the primary (but not the only) verification mechanism for software. Rather than waiting for some sort of calculus for software, we already have the tools at our disposal to ensure good engineering practices. Viewed in this light, we now have ammunition against managers who tell us "we don't have time to test." A bridge builder would never hear from his boss, "Don't bother doing structural analysis on that building—we have a tight deadline." The recognition that testing is indeed the path to reproducibility and quality in software allows us as developers to push back on arguments against it as professionally irresponsible.

Testing takes time, just like structural analysis takes time. Both activities ensure the quality of the end product. It's time for software developers to take up the mantle of responsibility for what they produce. Testing alone isn't sufficient, but it is necessary. Testing *is* the engineering rigor of software development.

Thinking in States

Niclas Nilsson

PEOPLE IN THE REAL WORLD HAVE A WEIRD RELATIONSHIP WITH STATE.
This morning, I stopped by the local store to prepare for another day of converting caffeine to code. Since my favorite way of doing that is by drinking lattes, and I couldn't find any milk, I asked the clerk.

"Sorry, we're super-duper, mega–out of milk."

To a programmer, that's an odd statement. You're either out of milk, or you're not. There is no scale when it comes to being out of milk. Perhaps she was trying to tell me that they'd be out of milk for a week, but the outcome was the same—espresso day for me.

In most real-world situations, people's relaxed attitude toward state is not an issue. Unfortunately, however, many programmers are quite vague about state, too—and that is a problem.

Consider a simple webshop that only accepts credit cards and does not invoice customers, with an `Order` class containing this method:

```
public boolean isComplete() {
    return isPaid() && hasShipped();
}
```

Reasonable, right? Well, even if the expression is nicely extracted into a method instead of copy 'n' pasted everywhere, the expression shouldn't exist at all. The fact that it does highlights a problem. Why? Because an order can't be shipped before it's paid. Thereby, `hasShipped` can't be true unless `isPaid` is true, which makes part of the expression redundant. You may still want `isComplete` for clarity in the code, but then it should look like this:

```
public boolean isComplete() {
    return hasShipped();
}
```

In my work, I see both missing checks and redundant checks all the time. This example is tiny, but when you add cancellation and repayment, it'll become more complex, and the need for good state handling increases. In this case, an order can only be in one of three distinct states:

- **In progress:** Can add or remove items. Can't ship.
- **Paid:** Can't add or remove items. Can be shipped.
- **Shipped:** Done. No more changes accepted.

These states are important, and you need to check that you're in the expected state before doing operations, and that you only move to a legal state from where you are. In short, you have to protect your objects carefully, in the right places.

But how do you begin thinking in states? Extracting expressions to meaningful methods is a very good start, but it is just a start. The foundation is to understand state machines. I know you may have bad memories from CS class, but leave them behind. State machines are not particularly hard. Visualize them to make them simple to understand and easy to talk about. Test-drive your code to unravel valid and invalid states and transitions and to keep them correct. Study the State pattern. When you feel comfortable, read up on Design by Contract. It helps you ensure a valid state by validating incoming data and the object itself on entry and exit of each public method.

If your state is incorrect, there's a bug, and you risk trashing data if you don't abort. If you find the state checks to be noise, learn how to use a tool, code generation, weaving, or aspects to hide them. Regardless of which approach you pick, thinking in states will make your code simpler and more robust.

Two Heads Are Often Better Than One

Adrian Wible

PROGRAMMING REQUIRES DEEP THOUGHT, and deep thought requires solitude. So goes the programmer stereotype.

This "lone wolf" approach to programming has been giving way to a more collaborative approach, which, I would argue, improves quality, productivity, and job satisfaction for programmers. This approach has developers working more closely with one another and also with nondevelopers—business and systems analysts, quality assurance professionals, and users.

What does this mean for developers? Being the expert technologist is no longer sufficient. You must become effective at working with others.

Collaboration is not about asking and answering questions or sitting in meetings. It's about rolling up your sleeves with someone else to jointly attack work.

I'm a big fan of pair programming. You might call this "extreme collaboration." As a developer, my skills grow when I pair. If I am weaker than my pairing partner in the domain or technology, I clearly learn from his or her experience. When I am stronger in some aspect, I learn more about what I know and don't know by having to explain myself. Invariably, we both bring something to the table and learn from each other.

When pairing, we each bring our collective programming experiences— domain as well as technical—to the problem at hand and can bring unique insight and experience into writing software effectively and efficiently. Even in cases of extreme imbalance in domain or technical knowledge, the more experienced participant invariably learns something from the other—perhaps a new keyboard shortcut, or exposure to a new tool or library. For the less-experienced member of the pair, this is a great way to get up to speed.

Pair programming is popular with, though not exclusive to, proponents of agile software development. Some who object to pairing ask, "Why should I pay two programmers to do the work of one?" My response is that, indeed, you should not. I argue that pairing increases quality, understanding of the domain and technology, and techniques (like IDE tricks), and mitigates the impact of lottery risk (one of your expert developers wins the lottery and quits the next day).

What is the long-term value of learning a new keyboard shortcut? How do we measure the overall quality improvement to the product resulting from pairing? How do we measure the impact of your partner not letting you pursue a dead-end approach to solving a difficult problem? One study cites an increase of 40% in effectiveness and speed.[*] What is the value of mitigating your "lottery risk"? Most of these gains are difficult to measure.

Who should pair with whom? If you're new to the team, it's important to find a team member who is knowledgeable. Just as important, find someone who has good interpersonal and coaching skills. If you don't have much domain experience, pair with a team member who is an expert in the domain.

If you are not convinced, experiment: collaborate with your colleagues. Pair on an interesting, gnarly problem. See how it feels. Try it a few times.

---

[*] J. T. Nosek, "The Case for Collaborative Programming," *Communications of the ACM*, March 1998

Two Wrongs Can Make a Right (and Are Difficult to Fix)

Allan Kelly

CODE NEVER LIES, BUT IT CAN CONTRADICT ITSELF. Some contradictions lead to those "How can that possibly work?" moments.

In an interview,[*] the principal designer of the Apollo 11 Lunar Module software, Allan Klumpp, disclosed that the software controlling the engines contained a bug that should have made the lander unstable. However, another bug compensated for the first, and the software was used for both Apollo 11 and 12 Moon landings before either bug was found or fixed.

Consider a function that returns a completion status. Imagine that it returns false when it should return true. Now imagine that the calling function neglects to check the return value. Everything works fine until one day someone notices the missing check and inserts it.

Or consider an application that stores state as an XML document. Imagine that one of the nodes is incorrectly written as TimeToLive instead of TimeToDie, as the documentation says it should. Everything appears fine while the writer code and the reader code both contain the same error. But fix one, or add a new application reading the same document, and the symmetry is broken, as well as the code.

When two defects in the code create one visible fault, the methodical approach to fixing faults can itself break down. The developer gets a bug report, finds the defect, fixes it, and retests. The reported fault still occurs, however, because a second defect is at work. So the first fix is removed, the code inspected until the second underlying defect is found, and a fix applied for that. But the first defect has returned, the reported fault is still seen, and so the second fix is rolled back. The process repeats, but now the developer has dismissed two possible fixes and is looking to make a third that will never work.

---

[*] *http://www.netjeff.com/humor/item.cgi?file=ApolloComputer*

The interplay between two code defects that appear as one visible fault not only makes it hard to fix the problem, but also leads developers down blind alleys, only to find they tried the right answers early on.

This doesn't happen only in code: the problem also exists in written requirements documents. And it can spread, virally, from one place to another. An error in the code compensates for an error in the written description.

It can spread to people, too: users learn that when the application says *Left*, it means *Right*, so they adjust their behavior accordingly. They even pass it on to new users: "Remember when that applications says 'click the left button,' it really means the button on the right." Fix the bug, and suddenly the users need retraining.

Single wrongs can be easy to spot and easy to fix. It is the problems with multiple causes, needing multiple changes, that are harder to resolve. In part, this is because easy problems are so easily fixed that people tend to fix them relatively quickly and store up the more difficult problems for a later date.

There is no simple advice for how to address faults arising from sympathetic defects. Awareness of the possibility, a clear head, and a willingness to consider all possibilities are needed.

Ubuntu Coding
for Your Friends

Aslam Khan

SO OFTEN, WE WRITE CODE IN ISOLATION and that code reflects our personal interpretation of a problem, as well as a very personalized solution. We may be part of the team, yet we are isolated, as is the team. We forget all too easily that this code created in isolation will be executed, used, extended, and relied upon by others. It is easy to overlook the social side of software creation. Creating software is a technical exercise mixed into a social exercise. We just need to lift our heads more often to realize that we are not working in isolation, and we have shared responsibility for increasing the probability of success for everyone, not just the development team.

You can write good-quality code in isolation, all the while lost in self. From one perspective, that is an egocentric approach (not *ego* as in arrogant, but *ego* as in personal). It is also a Zen view and it is about you, in that moment of creating code. I always try to live in the moment because it helps me get closer to good quality, but then I live in *my* moment. What about the moment of my team? Is my moment the same as the team's moment?

In Zulu, the philosophy of Ubuntu is summed up as "Umuntu ngumuntu ngabantu," which roughly translates to "A person is a person through (other) persons." I get better because you make me better through your good actions. The flip side is that you get worse at what you do when I am bad at what I do. Among developers, we can narrow it down to "A developer is a developer through (other) developers." If we take it down to the metal, then "Code is code through (other) code."

The quality of the code I write affects the quality of the code you write. What if my code is of poor quality? Even if you write very clean code, it is at the points where you use my code that your code quality will degrade to close to the quality of my code. You can apply many patterns and techniques to limit the damage, but the damage has already been done. I have caused you to do more than what you needed to do, simply because I did not think about you when I was living in my moment.

I may consider my code to be clean, but I can still make it better just by Ubuntu coding. What does Ubuntu code look like? It looks just like good, clean code. It is not about the code, the artifact. It is about the act of creating that artifact. Coding for your friends, with Ubuntu, will help your team live your values and reinforce your principles. The next person that touches your code, in whatever way, will be a better person and a better developer.

Zen is about the individual. Ubuntu is about Zen for a group of people. Very, very rarely do we create code for ourselves alone.

The Unix Tools
Are Your Friends

Diomidis Spinellis

IF, ON MY WAY TO EXILE ON A DESERT ISLAND, I had to choose between an IDE and the Unix toolchest, I'd pick the Unix tools without a second thought. Here are the reasons why you should become proficient with Unix tools.

First, IDEs target specific languages, while Unix tools can work with anything that appears in textual form. In today's development environment, where new languages and notations spring up every year, learning to work in the Unix way is an investment that will pay off time and again.

Furthermore, while IDEs offer just the commands their developers conceived, with Unix tools you can perform any task you can imagine. Think of them as (classic pre-Bionicle) Lego blocks: you create your own commands simply by combining the small but versatile Unix tools. For instance, the following sequence is a text-based implementation of Cunningham's signature analysis—a sequence of each file's semicolons, braces, and quotes, which can reveal a lot about the file's contents:

```
for i in *.java; do
    echo -n "$i: "
    sed 's/[^"{};]//g' $i | tr -d '\n'
    echo
done
```

In addition, each IDE operation you learn is specific to that given task—for instance, adding a new step in a project's debug build configuration. By contrast, sharpening your Unix tool skills makes you more effective at any task. As an example, I've employed the *sed* tool used in the preceding command sequence to morph a project's build for cross-compiling on multiple processor architectures.

Unix tools were developed in an age when a multiuser computer had 128KB of RAM. The ingenuity that went into their design means that nowadays they can handle huge data sets extremely efficiently. Most tools work like filters, processing just a single line at the time, meaning that there is no upper limit in the amount of data they can handle. You want to search for the number of edits stored in the half-terabyte English Wikipedia dump? A simple invocation of

```
grep '<revision>' | wc -l
```

will give you the answer without sweat. If you find a command sequence generally useful, you can easily package it into a shell script, using some uniquely powerful programming constructs, such as piping data into loops and conditionals. Even more impressively, Unix commands executing as pipelines, like the preceding one, will naturally distribute their load among the many processing units of modern multicore CPUs.

The small-is-beautiful provenance and open source implementations of the Unix tools make them ubiquitously available, even on resource-constrained platforms, like my set-top media player or DSL router. Such devices are unlikely to offer a powerful graphical user interface, but they often include the BusyBox application, which provides the most commonly used tools. And if you are developing on Windows, the Cygwin environment offers you all imaginable Unix tools, both as executables and in source code form.

Finally, if none of the available tools matches your needs, it's very easy to extend the world of the Unix tools. Just write a program (in any language you fancy) that plays by a few simple rules: your program should perform just a single task; it should read data as text lines from its standard input; and it should display its results unadorned by headers and other noise on its standard output. Parameters affecting the tool's operation are given in the command line. Follow these rules, and "yours is the Earth and everything that's in it."

Use the Right Algorithm and Data Structure

Jan Christiaan "JC" van Winkel

A big bank with many branch offices complained that the new computers it had bought for the tellers were too slow. This was in the time before everyone used electronic banking, and ATMs were not as widespread as they are now. People would visit the bank far more often, and the slow computers were making the people queue up. Consequently, the bank threatened to break its contract with the vendor.

The vendor sent a performance analysis and tuning specialist to determine the cause of the delays. He soon found one specific program running on the terminal that consumed almost all the CPU capacity. Using a profiling tool, he zoomed in on the program and he could see the function that was the culprit. The source code read:

```
for (i=0; i<strlen(s); ++i) {
    if (... s[i] ...) ...
}
```

And string s was, on average, thousands of characters long. The code (written by the bank) was quickly changed, and the bank tellers lived happily ever after....

SHOULDN'T THE PROGRAMMER have done better than to use code that needlessly scaled quadratically?

Each call to `strlen` traversed every one of the many thousand characters in the string to find its terminating null character. The string, however, never changed. By determining its length in advance, the programmer could have saved thousands of calls to `strlen` (and millions of loop executions):

```
n=strlen(s);
for (i=0; i<n; ++i) {
    if (... s[i] ...) ...
}
```

Everyone knows the adage "first make it work, then make it work fast" to avoid the pitfalls of micro-optimization. But the preceding example would almost make you believe that the programmer followed the Machiavellian adagio "first make it work slowly."

This thoughtlessness is something you may come across more than once. And it is not just a "don't reinvent the wheel" thing. Sometimes novice programmers just start typing away without really thinking, and suddenly they have "invented" bubble sort. They may even be bragging about it.

The other side of choosing the right algorithm is the choice of data structure. It can make a big difference: using a linked list for a collection of a million items you want to search through—compared to a hashed data structure or a binary tree—will have a big impact on the user's appreciation of your programming.

Programmers should not reinvent the wheel, and should use existing libraries where possible. But to be able to avoid problems like the bank's, they should also be educated about algorithms and how they scale. Is it just the eye candy in modern text editors that makes them as slow as old-school programs like WordStar in the 1980s? Many say reuse in programming is paramount. Above all, however, programmers should know when, what, and how to reuse. To do that, they should have knowledge of the problem domain and of algorithms and data structures.

A good programmer should also know when to use an abominable algorithm. For example, if the problem domain dictates that there can never be more than five items (like the number of dice in a *Yahtzee* game), you know that you always have to sort at most five items. In that case, bubble sort might actually be the most efficient way to sort the items. Every dog has its day.

So, read some good books—and make sure you understand them. And if you really read Donald Knuth's *The Art of Computer Programming* (Addison-Wesley Professional), well, you might even be lucky: find a mistake by the author, and you'll earn one of Don Knuth's hexadecimal dollar ($2.56) checks.

Verbose Logging
Will Disturb
Your Sleep

Johannes Brodwall

WHEN I ENCOUNTER A SYSTEM that has already been in development or production for a while, the first sign of real trouble is always a dirty log. You know what I'm talking about: when clicking a single link on a normal flow on a web page results in a deluge of messages in the only log that the system provides. Too much logging can be as useless as none at all.

If your systems are like mine, when your job is done, someone else's job is just starting. After the system has been developed, it will hopefully live a long and prosperous life serving customers (if you're lucky). How will you know if something goes wrong when the system is in production, and how will you deal with it?

Maybe someone monitors your system for you, or maybe you will monitor it yourself. Either way, the logs will probably be part of the monitoring. If something shows up and you have to be woken up to deal with it, you want to make sure there's a good reason for it. If my system is dying, I want to know. But if there's just a hiccup, I'd rather enjoy my beauty sleep.

For many systems, the first indication that something is wrong is a log message being written to some log. Mostly, this will be the error log. So do yourself a favor: make sure from day one that if something is logged in the error log, you're willing to have someone call and wake you in the middle of the night about it. If you can simulate load on your system during system testing, looking at a noise-free error log is also a good first indication that your system is reasonably robust—or an early warning if it's not.

Distributed systems add another level of complexity. You have to decide how to deal with an external dependency failing. If your system is very distributed, this may be a common occurrence. Make sure your logging policy takes this into account.

In general, the best indication that everything is all right is that the messages at a lower priority are ticking along happily. I want about one INFO-level log message for every significant application event.

A cluttered log is an indication that the system will be hard to control once it reaches production. If you don't expect anything to show up in the error log, it will be much easier to know what to do when something does show up.

WET Dilutes
Performance
Bottlenecks

Kirk Pepperdine

THE IMPORTANCE OF THE DRY PRINCIPLE (Don't Repeat Yourself) is that it codifies the idea that every piece of knowledge in a system should have a singular representation. In other words, knowledge should be contained in a single implementation. The antithesis of DRY is WET (Write Every Time). Our code is WET when knowledge is codified in several different implementations. The performance implications of DRY versus WET become very clear when you consider their numerous effects on a performance profile.

Let's start by considering a feature of our system, say *X*, that is a CPU bottleneck. Let's say feature *X* consumes 30% of the CPU. Now let's say that feature *X* has 10 different implementations. On average, each implementation will consume 3% of the CPU. As this level of CPU utilization isn't worth worrying about if we are looking for a quick win, it is likely that we'd miss that this feature is our bottleneck. However, let's say that we somehow recognized feature *X* as a bottleneck. We are now left with the problem of finding and fixing every single implementation. With WET, we have 10 different implementations that we need to find and fix. With DRY, we would clearly see the 30% CPU utilization and would have a tenth of the code to fix. And did I mention that we don't have to spend time hunting down each implementation?

There is one use case where we are often guilty of violating DRY: our use of collections. A common technique to implement a query would be to iterate over the collection and then apply the query in turn to each element:

```
public class UsageExample {
    private ArrayList<Customer> allCustomers = new ArrayList<Customer>();
    // ...
    public ArrayList<Customer> findCustomersThatSpendAtLeast(Money amount) {
        ArrayList<Customer> customersOfInterest = new ArrayList<Customer>();
        for (Customer customer: allCustomers) {
            if (customer.spendsAtLeast(amount))
```

```
        customersOfInterest.add(customer);
    }
    return customersOfInterest;
}
}
```

By exposing this raw collection to clients, we have violated encapsulation. This not only limits our ability to refactor, but it also forces users of our code to violate DRY by having each of them reimplement potentially the same query. This situation can easily be avoided by removing the exposed raw collections from the API. In this example, we can introduce a new, domain-specific collective type called CustomerList. This new class is more semantically in line with our domain. It will act as a natural home for all our queries.

Having this new collection type will also allow us to easily see if these queries are a performance bottleneck. By incorporating the queries into the class, we eliminate the need to expose representation choices, such as ArrayList, to our clients. This gives us the freedom to alter these implementations without fear of violating client contracts:

```
public class CustomerList {
    private ArrayList<Customer> customers = new ArrayList<Customer>();
    private SortedList<Customer> customersSortedBySpendingLevel =
            new SortedList<Customer)();
    // ...
    public CustomerList findCustomersThatSpendAtLeast(Money amount) {
        return new CustomerList(
                customersSortedBySpendingLevel.elementsLargerThan(amount));
    }
}
public class UsageExample {
    public static void main(String[] args) {
        CustomerList customers = new CustomerList();
        // ...
        CustomerList customersOfInterest =
                customers.findCustomersThatSpendAtLeast(someMinimalAmount);
        // ...
    }
}
```

In this example, adherence to DRY allowed us to introduce an alternate indexing scheme with SortedList keyed on our customers' level of spending. More important than the specific details of this particular example, following DRY helped us to find and repair a performance bottleneck that would have been more difficult to find had the code been WET.

When Programmers and Testers Collaborate

Janet Gregory

SOMETHING MAGICAL HAPPENS when testers and programmers start to collaborate. There is less time spent sending bugs back and forth through the defect tracking system. Less time is wasted trying to figure out whether something is really a bug or a new feature, and more time is spent developing good software to meet customer expectations. There are many opportunities for starting collaboration before coding even begins.

Testers can help customers write and automate acceptance tests using the language of their domain with tools such as Fit (Framework for Integrated Test). When these tests are given to the programmers before the coding begins, the team is practicing *acceptance test–driven development* (ATDD). The programmers write the fixtures to run the tests, and then code to make the tests pass. These tests then become part of the regression suite. When this collaboration occurs, the functional tests are completed early, allowing time for exploratory testing on edge conditions or through workflows of the bigger picture.

We can take it one step further. As a tester, I can supply most of my testing ideas before the programmers start coding a new feature. When I ask the programmers if they have any suggestions, they almost always provide me with information that helps me with better test coverage, or helps me to avoid spending a lot of time on unnecessary tests. Often, we have prevented defects because the tests clarify many of the initial ideas. For example, in one project I was on, the Fit tests I gave the programmers displayed the expected results of a query to respond to a wildcard search. The programmer had fully intended to code only complete word searches. We were able to talk to the customer and determine the correct interpretation before coding started. By collaborating, we prevented the defect, which saved us both a lot of wasted time.

Programmers can collaborate with testers to create successful automation as well. They understand good coding practices and can help testers set up a robust test automation suite that works for the whole team. I have often seen test automation projects fail because the tests are poorly designed. The tests try to test too much, or the testers haven't understood enough about the technology to be able to keep tests independent. The testers are often the bottleneck, so it makes sense for programmers to work with them on tasks like automation. Working with the testers to understand what can be tested early, perhaps by providing a simple tool, will give the programmers another cycle of feedback that will help them deliver better code in the long run.

When testers stop thinking that their only job is to break the software and find bugs in the programmers' code, programmers stop thinking that testers are "out to get them," and are more open to collaboration. When programmers start realizing that they are responsible for building quality into their code, testability of the code is a natural by-product, and the team can automate more of the regression tests together. The magic of successful teamwork begins.

Write Code As If You Had to Support It for the Rest of Your Life

Yuriy Zubarev

YOU COULD ASK 97 PEOPLE what every programmer should know and do, and you might get 97 distinct answers. This could be both overwhelming and intimidating at the same time. All advice is good, all principles are sound, and all stories are compelling, but where do you start? More important, once you have started, how do you keep up with all the best practices you've learned, and how do you make them an integral part of your programming practice?

I think the answer lies in your frame of mind or, more plainly, in your attitude. If you don't care about your fellow developers, testers, managers, sales and marketing people, and end users, then you will not be driven to employ test-driven development or write clear comments in your code, for example. I think there is a simple way to adjust your attitude and always be driven to deliver the best quality products:

Write code as if you had to support it for the rest of your life.

That's it. If you accept this notion, many wonderful things will happen. If you were to accept that any of your previous or current employers had the right to call you in the middle of the night, asking you to explain the choices you made while writing the fooBar method, you would gradually improve toward becoming an expert programmer. You would naturally want to come up with better variable and method names. You would stay away from blocks of code comprising hundreds of lines. You would seek, learn, and use design patterns. You would write comments, test your code, and refactor continually. Supporting all the code you'd ever written for the rest of your life should also be a scalable endeavor. You would therefore have no choice but to become better, smarter, and more efficient.

If you reflect on it, the code you wrote many years ago still influences your career, whether you like it or not. You leave a trail of your knowledge, attitude, tenacity, professionalism, level of commitment, and degree of enjoyment with every method, class, and module you design and write. People will form opinions about you based on the code that they see. If those opinions are constantly negative, you will get less from your career than you hoped. Take care of your career, of your clients, and of your users with every line of code—write code as if you had to support it for the rest of your life.

Write Small Functions Using Examples

Keith Braithwaite

WE WOULD LIKE TO WRITE CODE THAT IS CORRECT, and have evidence on hand that it is correct. It can help with both issues to think about the "size" of a function. Not in the sense of the amount of code that implements a function—although that is interesting—but rather the size of the mathematical function that our code manifests.

For example, in the game of *Go* there is a condition called *atari* in which a player's stones may be captured by her opponent: a stone with two or more free spaces adjacent to it (called *liberties*) is not in atari. It can be tricky to count how many liberties a stone has, but determining atari is easy if that is known. We might begin by writing a function like this:

```
boolean atari(int libertyCount)
    libertyCount < 2
```

This is larger than it looks. A mathematical function can be understood as a set, some subset of the Cartesian product of the sets that are its domain (here, `int`) and range (here, `boolean`). If those sets of values were the same size as in Java, then there would be `2L*(Integer.MAX_VALUE+(-1L*Integer.MIN_VALUE)+1L)` or 8,589,934,592 members in the set `int×boolean`. Half of these are members of the subset that is our function, so to provide complete evidence that our function is correct, we would need to check around 4.3×109 examples.

This is the essence of the claim that tests cannot prove the absence of bugs. Tests can demonstrate the presence of features, though. But still we have this issue of size.

The problem domain helps us out. The nature of *Go* means that the number of liberties of a stone is not any int, but exactly one of {1,2,3,4}. So we could alternatively write:

```
LibertyCount = {1,2,3,4}
boolean atari(LibertyCount libertyCount)
    libertyCount == 1
```

This is much more tractable: the function computed is now a set with at most eight members. In fact, four checked examples would constitute evidence of complete certainty that the function is correct. This is one reason why it's a good idea to use types closely related to the problem domain to write programs, rather than native types. Using domain-inspired types can often make our functions much smaller. One way to find out what those types should be is to find the examples to check in problem domain terms, before writing the function.

Write Tests
for People

Gerard Meszaros

YOU ARE WRITING AUTOMATED TESTS for some or all of your production code. Congratulations! You are writing your tests before you write the code? Even better!! Just doing this makes you one of the early adopters on the leading edge of software engineering practice. But are you writing good tests? How can you tell? One way is to ask, "Who am I writing the tests for?" If the answer is "For me, to save me the effort of fixing bugs" or "For the compiler, so they can be executed," then the odds are you aren't writing the best possible tests. So *who* should you be writing the tests for? For the person trying to understand your code.

Good tests act as documentation for the code they are testing. They describe how the code works. For each usage scenario, the test(s):

- Describe the context, starting point, or preconditions that must be satisfied

- Illustrate how the software is invoked

- Describe the expected results or postconditions to be verified

Different usage scenarios will have slightly different versions of each of these. The person trying to understand your code should be able to look at a few tests, and by comparing these three parts of the tests in question, be able to see what causes the software to behave differently. Each test should clearly illustrate the cause-and-effect relationship among these three parts.

This implies that what isn't visible in the test is just as important as what is visible. Too much code in the test distracts the reader with unimportant trivia. Whenever possible, hide such trivia behind meaningful method calls—the Extract Method refactoring is your best friend. And make sure you give each test a meaningful name that describes the particular usage scenario so the test reader doesn't have to reverse-engineer each test to understand what the various scenarios are. Between them, the names of the test class and class method should include at least the starting point and how the software is being invoked. This allows the test coverage to be verified via a quick scan of the method names. It can also be useful to include the expected results in the test method names as long as this doesn't cause the names to be too long to see or read.

It is also a good idea to test your tests. You can verify that they detect the errors you think they detect by inserting those errors into the production code (your own private copy that you'll throw away, of course). Make sure they report errors in a helpful and meaningful way. You should also verify that your tests speak clearly to a person trying to understand your code. The only way to do this is to have someone who isn't familiar with your code read your tests and tell you what she learned. Listen carefully to what she says. If she didn't understand something clearly, it probably isn't because she isn't very bright. It is more likely that you weren't very clear. (Go ahead and reverse the roles by reading her tests!)

You Gotta Care About the Code

Pete Goodliffe

IT DOESN'T TAKE SHERLOCK HOLMES to work out that good programmers write good code. Bad programmers...don't. They produce monstrosities that the rest of us have to clean up. You want to write the good stuff, right? You want to be a good programmer.

Good code doesn't pop out of thin air. It isn't something that happens by luck when the planets align. To get good code, you have to work at it. Hard. And you'll only get good code if you actually *care* about good code.

Good programming is not born from mere technical competence. I've seen highly intellectual programmers who can produce intense and impressive algorithms, who know their language standard by heart, but who write the most awful code. It's painful to read, painful to use, and painful to modify. I've seen more humble programmers who stick to very simple code, but who write elegant and expressive programs that are a joy to work with.

Based on my years of experience in the software factory, I've concluded that the real difference between adequate programmers and great programmers is this: *attitude*. Good programming lies in taking a professional approach, and wanting to write the best software you can, within the real-world constraints and pressures of the software factory.

The code to hell is paved with good intentions. To be an excellent programmer, you have to rise above good intentions, and actually *care* about the code—foster positive perspectives and develop healthy attitudes. Great code is carefully crafted by master artisans, not thoughtlessly hacked out by sloppy programmers or erected mysteriously by self-professed coding gurus.

You want to write good code. You want to be a good programmer. So, you care about the code:

- In any coding situation, you refuse to hack something that only *seems* to work. You strive to craft elegant code that is clearly correct (and has good tests to show that it is correct).

- You write code that is *discoverable* (that other programmers can easily pick up and understand), that is *maintainable* (that you, or other programmers, will be easily able to modify in the future), and that is *correct* (you take all steps possible to determine that you *have* solved the problem, not just made it look like the program works).

- You work well alongside other programmers. No programmer is an island. Few programmers work alone; most work in a team of programmers, either in a company environment or on an open source project. You consider other programmers and construct code that others can read. You want the team to write the best software possible, rather than to make yourself look clever.

- Any time you touch a piece of code, you strive to leave it better than you found it (either better structured, better tested, more understandable…).

- You care about code and about programming, so you are constantly learning new languages, idioms, and techniques. But you apply them only when appropriate.

Fortunately, you're reading this collection of advice because you do care about code. It interests you. It's your passion. Have fun programming. Enjoy cutting code to solve tricky problems. Produce software that makes you proud.

Your Customers Do Not Mean What They Say

Nate Jackson

I'VE NEVER MET A CUSTOMER YET that wasn't all too happy to tell me what they wanted—usually in great detail. The problem is that customers don't always tell you the whole truth. They generally don't lie, but they speak in customer speak, not developer speak. They use their terms and their contexts. They leave out significant details. They make assumptions that you've been at their company for 20 years, just like they have. This is compounded by the fact that many customers don't actually know what they want in the first place! Some may have a grasp of the "big picture," but they are rarely able to communicate the details of their vision effectively. Others might be a little lighter on the complete vision, but they know what they don't want. So, how can you possibly deliver a software project to someone who isn't telling you the whole truth about what they want? It's fairly simple. Just interact with them more.

Challenge your customers early, and challenge them often. Don't simply restate what they told you they wanted in their words. Remember: they didn't mean what they told you. I often implement this advice by swapping out the customer's words in conversation with them and judging their reaction. You'd be amazed how many times the term *customer* has a completely different meaning from the term *client*. Yet the guy telling you what he wants in his software project will use the terms interchangeably and expect you to keep track as to which one he's talking about. You'll get confused, and the software you write will suffer.

Discuss topics numerous times with your customers before you decide that you understand what they need. Try restating the problem two or three times with them. Talk to them about the things that happen just before or just after the topic you're talking about to get better context. If at all possible, have multiple people tell you about the same topic in separate conversations. They will almost always tell you different stories, which will uncover separate yet related facts. Two people telling you about the same topic will often contradict each other. Your best chance for success is to hash out the differences before you start your ultra-complex software crafting.

Use visual aids in your conversations. This could be as simple as using a whiteboard in a meeting, as easy as creating a visual mockup early in the design phase, or as complex as crafting a functional prototype. It is generally known that using visual aids during a conversation helps lengthen our attention span and increases the retention rate of the information. Take advantage of this fact and set your project up for success.

In a past life, I was a "multimedia programmer" on a team that produced glitzy projects. A client of ours described her thoughts on the look and feel of the project in great detail. The general color scheme discussed in the design meetings indicated a black background for the presentation. We thought we had it nailed. Teams of graphic designers began churning out hundreds of layered graphics files. Loads of time was spent molding the end product. On the day we showed the client the fruits of our labor, we got some startling news. When she saw the product, her exact words about the background color were, "When I said black, I meant white." So, you see, it is never as clear as black and white.

Contributors

Adrian Wible

 Adrian Wible's self-chosen title is "software development catalyst." He works for ThoughtWorks, Inc., mostly in project management roles, but strives to fend off suggestions of being "post-technical" by getting his hands dirty in software development from time to time. He was indoctrinated in the Waterfall/SDLC mode of development as a developer at IBM, and moved into project, people, and process management roles throughout his 20+ year career there and at Dell Computer Corporation. Adrian joined ThoughtWorks and discovered the Agile Manifesto (and XP, and Scrum, and…) in 2005, and realized that project work and management *could* be fun, exciting, and rewarding. He hasn't looked back since.

Adrian can be reached at *awible@thoughtworks.com*.

"Two Heads Are Often Better Than One," page 170

Alan Griffiths

 Alan Griffiths has been developing software through many fashions in development processes, technologies, and programming languages. During that time, he's delivered working software and development processes to a range of organizations, written for a number of magazines, spoken at several conferences, and made many friends. Firmly convinced that common sense is a rare and marketable commodity, he's currently working as an independent consultant through his company, Octopull Limited.

"Don't Rely on "Magic Happens Here"," page 58

Alex Miller

Alex Miller is a tech lead and engineer at Terracotta, Inc., the makers of the open source Java clustering product Terracotta. Prior to Terracotta, Alex worked at BEA Systems on the Aqua-Logic product line, and was chief architect at MetaMatrix. His interests include Java, concurrency, distributed systems, query languages, and software design.

Alex enjoys writing his blog at *http://tech.puredanger.com*. Along with the other members of the Terracotta team, he is a contributing author to the 2008 release *The Definitive Guide to Terracotta* (Apress). Alex is a frequent speaker at user groups and conferences, and is the founder of the Strange Loop conference in St. Louis (*http://thestrangeloop.com*).

"*Start from Yes,*" page 154

Allan Kelly

Allan Kelly is an accomplished software engineer who now works on the management side of development. He helps software teams improve their performance and adopt Agile methods. Based in London, he provides coaching, training, and consulting to companies large and small.

He is a frequent contributor to journals and conferences and is the author of *Changing Software Development: Learning to Be Agile* (John Wiley & Sons). Allan holds a BSc degree in computing and an MBA in management. He is currently working on a book of business strategy patterns for software companies. Find out more about Allan at *http://www.allankelly.net*.

"*Check Your Code First Before Looking to Blame Others,*" page 18

"*Two Wrongs Can Make a Right (and Are Difficult to Fix),*" page 172

Anders Norås

Anders Norås is a seasoned software developer and speaker. The "enterpriseyness" of EJB drove him to Microsoft .NET back in 2002. He quickly made a name for himself in the Microsoft community by using his Java experiences to get a head start on fellow developers. In 2006, he got reacquainted with his lost love—Java—and today he is a polyglot, combining the best of both worlds to build better software. Anders is the founder of the Quaere project and a contributor to a few open source projects. He has given talks at many conferences and user group meetings and is known for talks with few slides and lots of code. Anders lives in Norway, where he works for Objectware as its chief technology evangelist. You can read his blog at *http://andersnoras.com*.

"Don't Just Learn the Language, Understand Its Culture," page 54

Ann Katrin Gagnat

Ann Katrin Gagnat has four years of experience with Java and works as a system developer at Steria AS in Norway. Her professional interests include agile development, patterns, and writing readable code.

"Pair Program and Feel the Flow," page 128

Aslam Khan

Aslam Khan has spent more than half his life creating software. He still believes the truth is in the code that gets executed, but that belief is soberly balanced by his other core value—that people are more important than compilers. As a software architect and coach, Aslam spends his time helping teams to design and build better software, while having fun and making worthwhile friendships. Aslam is part of the factor10 team, and he is also an editor for the architecture community at DZone. You can read his blog at *http://aslamkhan.net*.

"Ubuntu Coding for Your Friends," page 174

Burk Hufnagel

Burk Hufnagel has been creating positive user experiences since 1978 as a software architect and developer. As someone who has spent most of his life designing and crafting software, Burk has made a habit of developing practical solutions for difficult problems. He is a bibliophile and a technophile, and tends to appreciate esoteric subjects.

Burk was one of the contributors to *97 Things Every Software Architect Should Know* (O'Reilly). He spoke at JavaOne 2008 on building better user experiences, and at the International Association of Software Architects' IT Architecture Regional Conference in 2007 and 2009. He also authored a paper for the IASA Skills Library on the not-so-subtle connection between user interface design and user experience.

"News of the Weird: Testers Are Your Friends," page 120

"Put the Mouse Down and Step Away from the Keyboard," page 138

Cal Evans

 Cal Evans is the director of the PCE for Ibuildings. He has been a programmer in various languages for more than 25 years. He is a published author of books and magazine articles on a variety of topics in several programming languages. He is an American currently based in Utrecht, the Netherlands, where he speaks, writes, codes, and works with the global PHP community. His blog can be found at *http://blog.calevans.com.*

> *"A Comment on Comments," page 32*
>
> *"Don't Touch That Code!," page 62*

Carroll Robinson

 Carroll Robinson is an embedded firmware engineer with approximately 20 years of experience. He has written C and assembly language firmware for a variety of processors (including 8051, 80x86, 68k, ARM7, and C2000), with applications in medical equipment, laboratory instrumentation, and wireless communications. He has written applications in C++, Java, and Python as well. He prefers to use open source tools (GCC, GAS, GDB) on Linux platforms, and has built several embedded Linux systems.

Carroll holds a master's of science degree in computer engineering from Case Western Reserve University in Cleveland, Ohio.

> *"Know How to Use Command-Line Tools," page 86*

Cay Horstmann

 Cay Horstmann grew up in northern Germany and attended the Christian-Albrechts-Universität in Kiel, a harbor town by the Baltic Sea. He received an MS in computer science from Syracuse University, and a PhD in mathematics from the University of Michigan in Ann Arbor. For four years, Cay was VP and CTO of an Internet startup that grew from three people in a tiny office to a public company. He now teaches computer science at San Jose State University. In his copious spare time, he writes books and articles on Java and computer science education.

> *"Step Back and Automate, Automate, Automate," page 156*

Chuck Allison

 Chuck Allison is an associate professor of computer science at Utah Valley University. He spent the two previous decades as a software engineer in the western U.S. He was an active contributor to C++98, senior editor of the *C/C++ Users Journal*, and coauthor of *Thinking in C++*, Volume 2, with Bruce Eckel. He was also the founder of *The C++ Source* and a contributing editor for *Better Software Magazine*. For more information, visit his website: *http://www.chuckallison.com*.

"Floating-Point Numbers Aren't Real," page 66

Clint Shank

 Clint Shank is a software developer, consultant, and mentor at Sphere of Influence, Inc., a company that leads with design-driven innovation to make curve-jumping, mouth-watering software that's awesome inside and out. His typical consulting focus is the design and construction of enterprise applications.

He is particularly interested in agile practices such as continuous integration and test-driven development; the programming languages Java, Groovy, Ruby, and Scala; frameworks like Spring and Hibernate; and general design and application architecture.

He keeps a blog at *http://clintshank.javadevelopersjournal.com/* and was a contributor to the book *97 Things Every Software Architect Should Know*.

"Continuous Learning," page 36

Dan Bergh Johnsson

 Dan Bergh Johnsson is senior consultant, partner, and official spokesperson for Omegapoint AB. He is a domain-driven design enthusiast and a long-time agile fan, and considers himself as part of the software craftsman tradition and the "OOPSLA School" of development. He cofounded the Swedish domain-driven design group DDD Sverige, contributes at *http://domaindrivendesign.org/*, and often delivers presentations at international conferences. He also shares his love of the craft in his blog, "Dear Junior: Letters to a Junior Programmer," which can be found at *http://dearjunior.blogspot.com*.

"Distinguish Business Exceptions from Technical," page 42
"Know Your Next Commit," page 94

Contributors

Dan North

Dan North writes software and coaches teams in agile and lean methods. He believes in putting people first and writing simple, pragmatic software. He also believes that most problems that teams face are about communication—and all the others are, too.

This is why he puts so much emphasis on "getting the words right," and why he is so passionate about behavior-driven development, communication, and how people learn. Dan has been working in the IT industry since he graduated in 1991, and he occasionally blogs at *http://dannorth.net*.

"Code in the Language of the Domain," page 22

Daniel Lindner

Daniel Lindner has developed software for over 15 years, both paid for and voluntary (open source). He cofounded a software development company in Karlsruhe, Germany, and gives lectures on software engineering. He has been seen having a social life, too.

"Let Your Project Speak for Itself," page 104

Diomidis Spinellis

Diomidis Spinellis is a professor in the department of management science and technology at the Athens University of Economics and Business, Greece. His research interests include software engineering, computer security, and programming languages. He has written the two award-winning *Open Source Perspective* books, *Code Reading* and *Code Quality* (both Addison-Wesley Professional), as well as dozens of scientific papers. His most recent work is the collection *Beautiful Architecture* (O'Reilly). He is a member of the IEEE Software editorial board, authoring the regular "Tools of the Trade" column. Diomidis is a FreeBSD committer and the developer of UMLGraph and other open source software packages, libraries, and tools. He holds an MEng in software engineering and a PhD in computer science, both from Imperial College London. Diomidis is a senior member of the ACM and the IEEE and a member of the Usenix Association.

"Large, Interconnected Data Belongs to a Database," page 96

"Put Everything Under Version Control," page 136

"The Unix Tools Are Your Friends," page 176

Edward Garson

 Edward Garson has been passionate about computing since learning to program in Logo on an Apple II. He currently works as an independent software development consultant, with a focus on helping companies transition to agile methods.

Edward's technical interests include software architecture and design, programming languages, and GNU/Linux. He is an enthusiastic presenter and has spoken at the British Computer Society, the Microsoft Architects Council, and various conferences. Edward is a contributing author of *97 Things Every Software Architect Should Know*.

Edward resides in Montreal with his wife and two sons. In his spare time, he enjoys skiing, climbing, and cycle touring.

"Apply Functional Programming Principles," page 4

Einar Landre

 Einar Landre is a practicing software professional with 25 years' experience as a developer, architect, manager, consultant, and author/presenter. He currently works for StatoilHydro's Business Application Services, where he engages in business-critical application development, architecture reviews, and software process improvement activities. Before joining StatoilHydro, Einar held positions as developer, consultant, and manager, working with the design and implementation of communication protocols, operating systems, and test software for the International Space Station. In recent years, he has become an active member of the professional community, authoring or coauthoring several papers presented at OOPSLA and SPE (Society of Petroleum Engineers). His professional interests include object-oriented programming, autonomous systems design, use of systems engineering practices, agile methodologies, and leadership in high-tech organizations.

Einar holds an MSc in information technology from the University of Strathclyde and is an IEEE-certified software development professional (CSDP). He lives with his family in Stavanger, Norway.

"Encapsulate Behavior, Not Just State," page 64
"Prefer Domain-Specific Types to Primitive Types," page 130

Filip van Laenen

Filip van Laenen is a chief engineer at the Norwegian software company Computas AS, which supplies IT solutions to the public and the private sector in Norway. He has over 10 years of experience in the software industry, from being a developer in both small and large teams to being the lead developer and compentency leader for security and software engineering for the whole company. In his professional career, he has used a number of programming languages, including Smalltalk, Java, Perl, Ruby, and PL/ SQL. He has a special interest in computer security and cryptography, and held the position of chief security officer at Computas for a number of years.

Filip holds an MSc in electronics and an MSc in computer science from the KULeuven. He comes originally from Flanders, but moved to Norway in 1997 and now lives with his family in Kolsås, near Oslo.

"Automate Your Coding Standard," page 8

Gerard Meszaros

Gerard Meszaros is an independent software development consultant, coach, and trainer with 25 years' experience building software and nearly a decade of experience applying agile methods such as Scrum, eXtreme Programming, and Lean. He speaks regularly at software development and testing conferences such as OOPSLA, Agile200x, and STAR. He is the author of *xUnit Test Patterns: Refactoring Test Code* (Addison-Wesley) and runs the website *http://xunitpatterns.com*.

"Write Tests for People," page 190

Giles Colborne

Giles Colborne has been working in usability for two decades at British Aerospace, Institute of Physics Publishing, and Euro RSCG group. In that time, he has spent hundreds of hours watching users in the lab and in the field. In 2004, he cofounded cxpartners, a usercentered design company that researches user behavior and designs user experiences for clients all over the world, including Nokia, Marriott, and eBay.

He was president of the UK Usability Professionals' Association from 2003 to 2007, and has worked with the British Standards Institute in developing standards and guidance on accessibility.

"Ask, "What Would the User Do?" (You Are Not the User)," page 6

"Prevent Errors," page 132

Giovanni Asproni

Giovanni Asproni is a freelance contractor and consultant living in the UK. Despite the fact that he often gets hired as an architect, team leader, trainer, and mentor, he is a programmer at heart, with a taste for simple code. He is a regular conference speaker, a member of the committee of the London XPDay conference, and the chair of the ACCU conference. Giovanni is a member of the ACCU, the AgileAlliance, the ACM, and the IEEE Computer Society.

> "Choose Your Tools with Care," page 20
>
> "Learn to Estimate," page 100

Greg Colvin

Greg Colvin has been hacking happily since 1972. When not cranking code or reading technical prose, he runs his dog on the beach or plays the blues in the local dives.

> "Know Your Limits," page 92

Gregor Hohpe

Gregor Hohpe is a software engineer with Google. He is best known for his thoughts on asynchronous messaging and service-oriented architectures, which he shares in a number of publications, including the seminal book *Enterprise Integration Patterns* (Addison-Wesley Professional). Find out more about his work at *http://www.eaipatterns.com*.

> "Convenience Is Not an -ility," page 38

Gudny Hauknes

Gudny Hauknes works as senior software developer at the Norwegian division of the consultancy company Steria. Since 1987, when she graduated from the Norwegian University of Technology (NTH/NTNU), she has had different roles within system development, project management, and quality assurance.

She is particularly interested in getting people to work together in a smooth way, having fun, working effectively, and, of course, making quality software.

> "Pair Program and Feel the Flow," page 128

Heinz Kabutz

Heinz Kabutz is the author of *The Java Specialists' Newsletter*, an advanced Java publication read by 50,000 Java specialists in 120 countries. Most of Heinz's time is spent writing Java code as a contractor for a number of companies. In addition, he lectures companies on how to write more effective Java, taking advantage of its advanced features.

Heinz is a Java Champion and was interviewed by Sun Microsystems (see *http://java.sun.com/developer/technicalArticles/Interviews/community/kabutz_qa.html*).

"Know Your IDE," page 90

Jan Christiaan "JC" van Winkel

JC van Winkel is a trainer and courseware developer for the small Dutch training and consulting company AT Computing. His work focuses on UNIX/Linux (system administration, security, performance analysis) and programming languages (mostly C, C++, and Python). He is also the Dutch representative for C++ standardization. JC was a board member of the Netherlands Unix User's group (NLUUG) for 12 years, during 6 of which he also served as chair.

"Use the Right Algorithm and Data Structure," page 178

Janet Gregory

The coauthor of *Agile Testing: A Practical Guide for Agile Testers and Teams* (Addison-Wesley Professional), Janet Gregory is a consultant who specializes in helping teams build quality systems using agile methods. Based in Calgary, Canada, Janet's greatest passion is promoting agile quality processes. As tester or coach, she has helped introduce agile development practices into companies and has successfully transitioned several traditional test teams into the agile world. Her focus is working with business users and testers to understand their roles in agile projects. Janet teaches courses on agile testing and is a frequent speaker at agile and testing software conferences around the world. Read more at *http://janetgregory.ca*.

"When Programmers and Testers Collaborate," page 184

Jason P. Sage

 Jason P. Sage is a computer consultant and business owner whose primary focus is system design, integration, customer relationship management (CRM), original server software, data processing, and 3D graphics software. Jason is a true programming enthusiast; he got his start in 1981, when he was 10 years old, on a Timex Sinclair with 2k of memory and a cassette recorder. Since then, he has written all sorts of software, ranging from video games and an operating system to a warehouse management system that runs one of the nation's largest natural food distributors.

He is often engaged in online forums, assisting and teaching fellow programmers and students of all ages.

"Reinvent the Wheel Often," page 144

Johannes Brodwall

 Johannes Brodwall is chief scientist at the Norwegian division of the consulting company Steria. He likes to take a broad view of projects to understand how multiple disciplines and technologies can together (hopefully) create value for users of software systems. He organizes activities in the Oslo agile community. His two most time-consuming activities are the Oslo Extreme Programming Meetup and the annual Smidig 200x conferences, a Norwegian-language agile conference (*smidig* is the Norwegian word for "agile"). He is a regular speaker at events in the Oslo area and writes frequently about software development in his blog at *http://johannesbrodwall.com*.

"Keep the Build Clean," page 84
"Verbose Logging Will Disturb Your Sleep," page 180

Jon Jagger

 Jon Jagger is a self-employed software consultant/trainer/programmer/mentor/enthusiast, etc., specializing in agile software development (people and process), test-driven development, UML, design, analysis, OO, and curly-bracket languages (C#, C, C++, Java). He is a UK C panel member and a lapsed UK C++ panel member, and served as the convenor and Principal UK Expert (PUKE!) for C#'s ECMA standardization.

Jon is also the inventor of the *Average Time To Green* game. He has had numerous articles published both online and in magazines and is the coauthor of

---

two books: *Microsoft® Visual C#® .NET Step by Step* (Microsoft Press) and *C# Annotated Standard* (Morgan Kaufmann).

Jon is married to the beautiful Natalie, and is the proud father of Ellie, Penny, and Patrick. He is also a mad keen freshwater fisherman.

"Do Lots of Deliberate Practice," page 44

"Make the Invisible More Visible," page 112

Jørn Ølmheim

Jørn Ølmheim is a practicing software professional with over 10 years of experience as a developer, architect, and author/presenter. He currently works for Statoil, developing software for a number of research projects, mostly using Java, Ruby, and Python with a pinch of Fortran and C/C++ for high-performance computing. His main interests include agile practices with an emphasis on developer craftsmanship, programming languages, and autonomous systems.

In his spare time, he enjoys skiing, mountain biking, and spending time with his family.

"Beauty Is in Simplicity," page 10

Kari Røssland

Kari Røssland is a software developer at the Norwegian division of the consulting company Steria. In the three years since she got her master's degree in computer science from NTNU in Trondheim, Norway, she has worked on several different projects. She is particularly interested in agile development and is passionate about efficient, joyful cooperation between participants in software projects.

"Pair Program and Feel the Flow," page 128

Karianne Berg

Karianne Berg holds an MSc from University of Bergen, Norway, and is currently employed at the Norwegian consulting firm Objectware. She likes to contribute to making people better developers, and is co-organizer of the ROOTS and Smidig conferences, as well as the Oslo XP Meetup. She has also presented at several conferences, and was last seen at Smidig 2009. Karianne's main fields of interest include agile development, patterns, and the Spring framework.

"Read Code," page 140

Keith Braithwaite

Keith Braithwaite is a principal consultant with Zuhlke. He also manages its Centre of Agile Practice. This group provides training, coaching, mentoring, toolsmithing, and straightforward development to enhance client teams' capabilities. He has maintained compilers, modeled GSM networks, and ported sat-nav sytems for startups, product companies, and global service organizations. He has earned money writing code in C, C++, Java, Python, and Smalltalk. Keith increasingly focuses on the use of "checked examples" or "automated tests" as effective tools for requirements gathering and analysis, system design, and project management.

His blog is at *http://peripateticaxiom.blogspot.com/*; find his conference presentations at *http://www.keithbraithwaite.demon.co.uk/professional/presentations/*.

"Read the Humanities," page 142

"Write Small Functions Using Examples," page 188

Kevlin Henney

Kevlin Henney is an independent consultant and trainer. His work focuses on patterns and architecture, programming techniques and languages, and development process and practice. He has been a columnist for various magazines and online publications, including *The Register, Better Software, Java Report, CUJ,* and *C++ Report.* Kevlin is coauthor of two volumes in the *Pattern-Oriented Software Architecture* series: *A Pattern Language for Distributed Computing* and *On Patterns and Pattern Languages* (Wiley). He also contributed to *97 Things Every Software Architect Should Know.*

"Comment Only What the Code Cannot Say," page 34

"Test for Required Behavior, Not Incidental Behavior," page 160

"Test Precisely and Concretely," page 162

Kirk Pepperdine

Kirk Pepperdine works as an independent consultant offering Java performance-related services. Prior to focusing on Java, Kirk developed and tuned systems written in C/C++, Smalltalk, and a variety of other languages. Kirk has written many articles and spoken at several conferences on the subject of performance tuning.

He helped evolve *http://www.javaperformancetuning.com* as a resource for performance-tuning tips and information.

"Missing Opportunities for Polymorphism," page 118

"The Road to Performance Is Littered with Dirty Code Bombs," page 148

"WET Dilutes Performance Bottlenecks," page 182

Klaus Marquardt

Klaus Marquardt's software development experience covers life-support systems, international projects, frameworks and product lines, and agility in regulated environments. He has documented a series of diagnoses and therapies on software systems that stem from his interest in the mutual influences of technology, humans, processes, and organization; these can be found at *http://www.sustainable-architecture.eu*. Furthermore, he enjoys writing patterns, running conference sessions that explore new ground, and having a life beyond software.

"Learn Foreign Languages," page 98

"The Longevity of Interim Solutions," page 108

Linda Rising

Linda Rising has a PhD from Arizona State University and a background that includes university teaching and industry work in a variety of domains. An internationally known presenter on patterns, retrospectives, agile development, and the change process, Linda has authored numerous articles and four books, the most recent, *Fearless Change: Patterns for Introducing New Ideas* (Addison-Wesley), with Mary Lynn Manns.

"A Message to the Future," page 116

Marcus Baker

Marcus Baker is a happy programmer who's astonished that he gets paid for it. The joy extends to telephony, data mining, robotics, and web development. He is also an occasional writer and columnist, and sometimes organizer of user groups and conferences. Today, though, he has to look after the kids.

"Install Me," page 80

Matt Doar

Matt Doar is a consultant working with software tools such as version control (CVS, Subversion), build systems (make, SCons), and bug trackers (Bugzilla, JIRA). Most of his clients are smaller startups in Silicon Valley. Matt is also the author of O'Reilly's *Practical Development Environments*.

"How to Use a Bug Tracker," page 76

Mattias Karlsson

Mattias Karlsson spends most of his time working with software development in the financial sector as well as leading a Java User Group in Stockholm, Sweden. Mattias has worked with OO software development since 1993. Through the years, he has gained experience in many different roles, including developer, architect, team leader, coach, manager, and teacher. In these roles, he receives consistent feedback about his ability to inspire and motivate the people he works with. The JUG holds six to eight fully booked meetings per year, with more then 200 participants at every meeting. Mattias is also one of the organizers behind Jfokus. Jfokus is the largest Java-focused annual conference in Stockholm.

In his spare time, Mattias can be found playing with his children or riding his motorcycle, as well as changing underprivileged people's lives by building houses with Habitat for Humanity. Mattias also supports Kiva, a person-to-person microloan organization. Join his effort to improve the world at *http://www.kiva.org/team/jug*.

"Code Reviews," page 28

Michael Feathers

Michael Feathers is a consultant with Object Mentor International. He balances his time between working with, training, and coaching various teams around the world. Michael developed CppUnit, the initial port of JUnit to C++, and FitCpp, a C++ port of the Fit integrated-test framework. Michael is also the author of the book *Working Effectively with Legacy Code* (Prentice Hall).

"The Golden Rule of API Design," page 70

Michael Hunger

Michael Hunger has been passionate about software development since his childhood days in East Germany. He is particularly interested in the people who develop software, software craftsmanship, programming languages, and improving code. While he likes coaching and in-project development as an independent consultant ("better software development evangelist"—*http://jexp.de*), he really enjoys the numerous other projects in his life.

One half of his life is devoted to his family of three kids, a longtime obsession with a text-based multiuser dungeon (MUD MorgenGrauen), reading books whenever possible, running his coffee shop "die-buchbar" with a workshop for printing on things, and tinkering with and without Lego®. The other half is filled with working with programming languages and learning new ones, enjoying IT podcasts (especially Software Engineering Radio; *http://se-radio.net/*), participating in exciting and ambitious projects like qi4j, creating DSLs (jequel, squill, and xmldsl), lots of refactoring, and contributing to and reviewing books in progress. Recently, he started to present at conferences.

"Domain-Specific Languages," page 46

Mike Lewis

Mike Lewis is currently a software engineer at Lutron Electronics, and an independent software consultant in his spare time. He applies over a decade of software engineering experience toward designing elegant and intuitive software solutions. He is a process improvement advocate whose passion lies in enhancing the user experience of absolutely everything.

Mike holds a BS and an MS in computer engineering, both from the Rochester Institute of Technology. Mike currently resides in Allentown, Pennsylvania, just outside of New York City and Philadelphia.

"Don't Be Afraid to Break Things," page 48

Nate Jackson

Nate Jackson is a senior software architect in Buffalo, New York. He has been writing code of one kind or another since 1979, when he got his TI-99 and a basic emulator cartridge. By following his own advice, he has satisfied all of his customers—even the lady who wanted the white background.

"Your Customers Do Not Mean What They Say," page 194

Neal Ford

Neal Ford is software architect and meme wrangler at Thought-Works, a global IT consultancy with an exclusive focus on end-to-end software development and delivery. He is the designer/developer of applications, instructional materials, magazine articles, courseware, video/DVD presentations, and author and/or editor of five books. He also speaks at lots of conferences. You can assuage your ravenous curiosity about Neal at *http://www.nealford.com*.

"Testing Is the Engineering Rigor of Software Development," page 166

Niclas Nilsson

Niclas Nilsson is a software development coach, consultant, educator, and writer with a deep passion for the craft and a love of good design and architecture. He began working as a developer in 1992. From his experience, he knows that some choices in software development—like languages, tools, communication, and processes—make a significant difference. This is the reason behind his affection for dynamic languages, test-driven development, code generation, metaprogramming, and agile processes. Niclas is a cofounder of factor10, and he is also an editor for the architecture community at InfoQ. Niclas blogs at *http://niclasnilsson.se*.

"Thinking in States," page 168

Olve Maudal

Olve Maudal lives in Norway. Married. Two kids. Dedicated computer geek. These days, mostly coding in C and C++.

At university, he studied software engineering and artificial intelligence. His professional career started in an oil service company developing systems for finding oil and gas. He then spent a few years developing systems for moving money. Now he works for a telecom company developing systems for effective communication between people.

Olve is an active member of the vibrant geek community in Oslo, where, among other things, he organizes the Oslo C++ Users Group. You can read his blog at *http://olvemaudal.wordpress.com*.

"Hard Work Does Not Pay Off," page 74

Paul W. Homer

Paul W. Homer is a software developer, writer, and occasional photographer, who was drawn into software development several decades ago and has been struggling ever since with trying to build increasingly complex systems. His experience includes in-house, consulting, and commercial development from a diverse array of concurrent posisions including analyst, architect, programmer, manager, and even—foolishly—CTO. He is willing to play any role that is focused on getting systems built and released.

Over the last few years, he has turned more of his attention toward communicating with his fellow developers, including a self-published book, blogging, and way too much commenting in the hopes of helping an industry rationalize itself and reach new heights.

"Simplicity Comes from Reduction," page 150

Pete Goodliffe

Pete Goodliffe is a software developer, columnist, speaker, and author who never stays at the same place in the software food chain. He's worked in numerous languages on diverse projects. He also teaches and mentors programmers, and writes the regular "Professionalism in Programming" column for ACCU's *CVu* magazine (*http://accu.org/*).

Pete's popular book, *Code Craft* (No Starch Press), is a practical and entertaining investigation of the entire programming pursuit. Pete enjoys writing excellent, bug-free code, so he can spend more time having fun with his kids. He has a passion for curry and doesn't wear shoes.

"Don't Ignore That Error!," page 52

"Improve Code by Removing It," page 78

"You Gotta Care About the Code," page 192

Peter Sommerlad

Peter Sommerlad is professor and head of the Institute for Software at HSR Rapperswil. Peter is coauthor of *Pattern-Oriented Software Architecture*, Volume 1, and *Security Patterns* (both Wiley). His long-term goal is to make software simpler through *decremental development*: refactoring software down to 10% of its size with better architecture, testability, quality, and functionality.

"Only the Code Tells the Truth," page 124

Rajith Attapattu

Rajith Attapattu is a senior software engineer on Red Hat's MRG team. Rajith is an open source enthusiast and has been a contributor on several Apache projects, including Apache Qpid, Apache Synapse, Apache Tuscany, and Apache Axis2. His recent focus has been on building scalable and reliable messaging middleware, and he is part of the AMQP (Advanced Message Queuing Protocol) working group.

He has published several articles and spoken at several conferences and user groups, including ApacheCon, Colorado Software Summit, and Toronto JUG. Rajith's research interests are in improving scalability and high availability of distributed systems. Rajith enjoys painting and playing cricket during his free time.

Rajith can be reached at *rajith@apache.org*, and he maintains a presence at *http://rajith.2rlabs.com*.

> *"Before You Refactor,"* page 12
>
> *"Test While You Sleep (and over Weekends),"* page 164

Randy Stafford

Randy Stafford is a practicing software professional with 20 years' experience as a developer, analyst, architect, manager, consultant, and author/presenter. He's currently a member of Oracle's A-Team, where he's involved with POC projects, architecture reviews, and production crises. He specializes in grid, SOA, performance, HA, and JEE/ORM work.

Randy has been technical advisor to Rally Software, chief architect of IQNavigator, director of development at SynXis, consultant for GemStone and Smalltalk, and a simulation specialist in the aerospace and CASE industries. He's contributed to *97 Things Every Software Architect Should Know, Patterns of Enterprise Application Architecture* (Wiley), and *EJB Design Patterns* (Addison-Wesley Professional).

> *"Interprocess Communication Affects Application Response Time,"* page 82

Richard Monson-Haefel

Richard Monson-Haefel, an independent software developer, has coauthored all five editions of *Enterprise JavaBeans* and both editions of *Java Message Service* (both from O'Reilly), and authored *J2EE Web Services* (Addison-Wesley). Richard is the editor of *97 Things Every Software Architect Should Know*. He cofounded the OpenEJB open source project, the EJB container for Apache Geronimo, and currently consults as an iPhone and Microsoft Surface developer.

"Fulfill Your Ambitions with Open Source," page 68

Robert C. Martin (Uncle Bob)

 Robert C. Martin (Uncle Bob) has been a software professional since 1970 and is founder and president of Object Mentor, Inc., in Gurnee, Illinois. Object Mentor, Inc., is an international firm of highly experienced software developers and managers who specialize in helping companies get their projects done. Object Mentor offers process improvement consulting, object-oriented software design consulting, training, and skill development services to major corporations worldwide.

Bob has published dozens of articles in various trade journals, and is a regular speaker at international conferences and trade shows. He has authored and edited many books, including *Designing Object-Oriented C++ Applications Using the Booch Method* (Prentice Hall), *Patterns Languages of Program Design 3* (Addison-Wesley Professional), *More C++ Gems* (Cambridge University Press), *Extreme Programming in Practice* (Addison-Wesley Professional), *Agile Software Development: Principles, Patterns, and Practices, UML for Java Programmers*, and *Clean Code* (all Prentice Hall).

A leader in the industry of software development, Bob served three years as the editor-in-chief of the *C++ Report*, and he served as the first chairman of the Agile Alliance.

"The Boy Scout Rule," page 16

"The Professional Programmer," page 134

"The Single Responsibility Principle," page 152

Rod Begbie

 Rod Begbie originally hails from Scotland, but currently leaves his heart in San Francisco.

His day job is engineering lead and panda wrangler at Slide, Inc. Previously, he was employed as an API architect at Current TV, lurked in the R&D labs of Bose Corporation, consulted with Sapient, and ducked out the (first) dot-com bubble-burst in the basement of a bank, building systems for fixed-income annuity analysis, which is as dull as it sounds.

"Don't Be Cute with Your Test Data," page 50

Russel Winder

Russel Winder is a partner in Concertant LLP, which provides analysis and consultancy on all aspects of parallelism, concurrency, and multicore systems. He is also an independent consultant, author, and trainer on programming, programming languages (Java, Groovy, and Python), version control systems (Subversion, Bazaar, and Git) and build frameworks (Gant, SCons, Gradle, Ant, and Maven). Russel is author of *Developing C++ Software* (Wiley), and coauthor of *Developing Java Software* (Wiley) and *Python for Rookies* (Cengage Learning Business Press).

"Know Well More Than Two Programming Languages," page 88

"Message Passing Leads to Better Scalability in Parallel Systems," page 114

Ryan Brush

Ryan Brush is a director and Distinguished Engineer with Cerner Corporation, where he has worked since 1999. He is primarily interested in the application of technology to healthcare.

"Code Is Design," page 24

"The Guru Myth," page 72

Sam Saariste

Sam Saariste has an MSc degree in electrical engineering and has been developing software professionally since 1995. He has done so in a variety of application areas, ranging from real-time speech processing solutions for telecoms to financial trading applications for investment banking. His language of choice is C++, and he has been a member of the BSI C++ panel since 2005. Sam has been a fan of agile development methods since he discovered XP around 2000. He cares about high-quality software and believes that with agile and lean, both higher quality and higher productivity can be achieved simultaneously.

"Resist the Temptation of the Singleton Pattern," page 146

Sarah Mount

Sarah Mount is a senior lecturer in computer science at the University of Wolverhampton. Her interests lie in the area of programming languages and tools, especially for wireless sensor networks and other distributed systems. She has taught introductory programming to undergraduate students for nine years and is a coauthor of the textbook *Python for Rookies* (Cengage Learning Business Press).

"Take Advantage of Code Analysis Tools," page 158

Scott Meyers

 Scott Meyers is an author, trainer, speaker, and consultant with over three decades of experience in software development practice and research. He's authored dozens of journal and magazine articles, as well as the books *Effective C++*, *More Effective C++*, and *Effective STL* (all Addison-Wesley Professional). He also designed and oversaw their electronic publication in HTML and PDF forms. Scott is consulting editor for Addison-Wesley's *Effective Software Development* series and was an inaugural member of the advisory board for the online journal, *The C++ Source* (*http://www.artima.com/cppsource*). He received his PhD in computer science from Brown University. His website is *http://www.aristeia.com/*.

"Make Interfaces Easy to Use Correctly and Hard to Use Incorrectly," page 110

Seb Rose

 Seb Rose is a principal software engineer working on the Rational DOORS team in Edinburgh. He first worked as a programmer in 1980 writing applications for estate agents and solicitors in compiled BASIC on an Apple IIe. Upon graduating from Edinburgh University in 1987, he worked on the REKURSIV project before becoming a freelance contractor. Today, his primary software interests are agile practices and the resuscitation of legacy code.

"Act with Prudence," page 2

Steve Berczuk

 Steve Berczuk is a software engineer at Humedica, where he develops business intelligence solutions for the healthcare industry. He has been developing software applications for over 20 years, and is the author of *Software Configuration Management Patterns: Effective Teamwork, Practical Integration* (Addison-Wesley Professional). In addition to developing software, he enjoys helping teams deliver more effectively through the use of agile methods and software configuration management. His website is *http://www.berczuk.com*.

"Deploy Early and Often," page 40
"Own (and Refactor) the Build," page 126

Steve Freeman

 Steve Freeman is an independent consultant specializing in agile software development. He has led, coached, and trained teams around the world. He is coauthor of the book *Growing Object-Oriented Software, Guided by Tests* (Addison-Wesley). Steve is one of the 2006 winners of the Agile Alliance Gordon Pask award. He is a committer to the jMock and Hamcrest projects, and was an author of NMock. He is a founder member of the eXtreme Tuesday Club and was chair of the first London XpDay. Steve has been an organizer and presenter at many international industry conferences. Steve has a PhD from the University of Cambridge and, in previous lives, took degrees in statistics and music. These days, he is interested in writing better code and exploring organizational complexity.

"*Code Layout Matters*," page 26

"*One Binary*," page 122

Steve Smith

 Steve Smith is a software developer, speaker, author, and mentor. He has worked in the software development world professionally since 1997 and has contributed to several books, primarily in the ASP.NET space. He is a regular speaker at user groups and industry conferences like DevConnections and Microsoft TechEd. Steve is also a former U.S. Army Engineer Captain and a veteran of Operation Iraqi Freedom, where the platoon he led was involved in clearing unexploded munitions and IEDs. Steve lives in Ohio with his wife and two children, and is one of the coordinators of the Hudson Software Craftsmanship group in Hudson, Ohio.

"*Don't Repeat Yourself*," page 60

Thomas Guest

 Thomas Guest is an experienced and enthusiastic computer programmer. He prefers high-level languages and simple solutions. His writing has been published in a number of online and print magazines as well as on his own site, *http://www.wordaligned.org*.

"*Learn to Say, "Hello, World"*," page 102

Udi Dahan

 Udi Dahan is The Software Simplist, an internationally renowned expert on software architecture and design. A solutions architecture and connected systems MVP for four consecutive years, Udi is also one of 33 experts in Europe recognized by the International .NET Association, an author and trainer for the International Association of Software Architects, and an SOA, Web Services, and XML Guru recommended by DDJ.

When not consulting, speaking, or training, Udi leads the development of NServiceBus, the most popular open source .NET enterprise service bus. He can be contacted via his blog at *http://www.UdiDahan.com.*

"Beware the Share," page 14

Verity Stob

 Verity Stob is the pseudonym of a programmer based in London, England. Although she professes competence in C++ and the usual curly-bracketed scripting languages, and designs and writes code for a number of platforms, she is probably at her happiest and does least harm when she is making Windows programs in CodeGear's Delphi.

For over 20 years, Verity has written supposedly amusing articles and columns for various magazines, newspapers, and websites, including the legendary (i.e., long-defunct) *.EXE Magazine*, the mold-breaking (i.e., more recently defunct) *Dr. Dobb's Journal*, and the scurrilous (i.e., actually profitable) *The Register*. In 2005, she published a collection of these pieces as *The Best of Verity Stob* (Apress), and so achieved a lifetime's ambition—to be paid twice for the same work.

Verity regards her entry in Wikipedia as a travesty of brevity.

"Don't Nail Your Program into the Upright Position," page 56

Walter Bright

 Walter Bright is a compiler writer, having implemented compilers for C, C++, ECMAScript, ABEL, Java, and, most recently, the D programming language. Walter is also known for inventing the *Empire* strategy game.

"The Linker Is Not a Magical Program," page 106

Yechiel Kimchi

 Yechiel Kimchi is a mathematician (PhD in abstract set theory, Hebrew University, Jerusalem), a computer scientist (teaching more than 10 years with the CS faculty at The Technion, Israel), and a software developer—spending more than 15 years alternating between working for big high-tech companies and working as a consultant through his own small firm. Working initially in C, and then in C++, he is interested in object orientation and the ways to develop software that is correct, maintainable, and efficient at the same time. Among other things, he developed heuristics for efficiently solving practical NP-hard problems, but he considers as his greatest achievement the influence he had on the technical education of several thousand Israeli software engineers.

"Coding with Reason," page 30

Yuriy Zubarev

 Yuriy Zubarev is a software architect and team lead with YachtWorld.com, a division of Dominion Enterprises. His work focuses on integration of software systems, knowledge gathering and tracking techniques, and increasing the technical efficiency and proficiency of his company. Yuriy lives and works in beautiful Vancouver city in British Columbia, Canada. When he isn't writing code, you can often find him Latin dancing.

"Write Code As If You Had to Support It for the Rest of Your Life," page 186

Index

W

WET (Write Every Time), 182–183
What is Software Design?, 166
Wible, Adrian
    biography, 196
    Two Heads Are Often Better Than
        One, 170–171
Winder, Russel
    biography, 216
    Know Well More Than Two
        Programming Languages, 88–89
    Message Passing Leads to Better
        Scalability in Parallel Systems,
        114–115
Wittgenstein, Ludwig, 142
working together, 154–155, 170–171
    collaboration between testers and
        programmers, 184–185
    customers' requests, 194
working too hard, 74–75, 138–139

X

XFDs (extreme feedback device), 104–105
XML, 47

Y

yes, starting at, 154–155

Z

Zubarev, Yuriy
    biography, 220
    Write Code As If You Had to Support
        It for the Rest of Your Life,
        186–187

Colophon

The cover and heading font is Gotham; the text font is Minion Pro; and the code font is TheSansMonoCondensed.

Buy this book and get access to the online edition for 45 days—for free!

97 Things Every Programmer Should Know

Edited by Kevlin Henney
January 2010, $29.99
ISBN 9780596809485

With Safari Books Online, you can:

Access the contents of thousands of technology and business books

- Quickly search over 7000 books and certification guides
- Download whole books or chapters in PDF format, at no extra cost, to print or read on the go
- Copy and paste code
- Save up to 35% on O'Reilly print books
- **New!** Access mobile-friendly books directly from cell phones and mobile devices

Stay up-to-date on emerging topics before the books are published

- Get on-demand access to evolving manuscripts.
- Interact directly with authors of upcoming books

Explore thousands of hours of video on technology and design topics

- Learn from expert video tutorials
- Watch and replay recorded conference sessions

To try out Safari and the online edition of this book FREE for 45 days, go to **www.oreilly.com/go/safarienabled** and enter the coupon code PUZNJFH. To see the complete Safari Library, visit safari.oreilly.com.

Spreading the knowledge of innovators   safari.oreilly.com

LaVergne, TN USA
07 February 2011
215577LV00012B/7/P